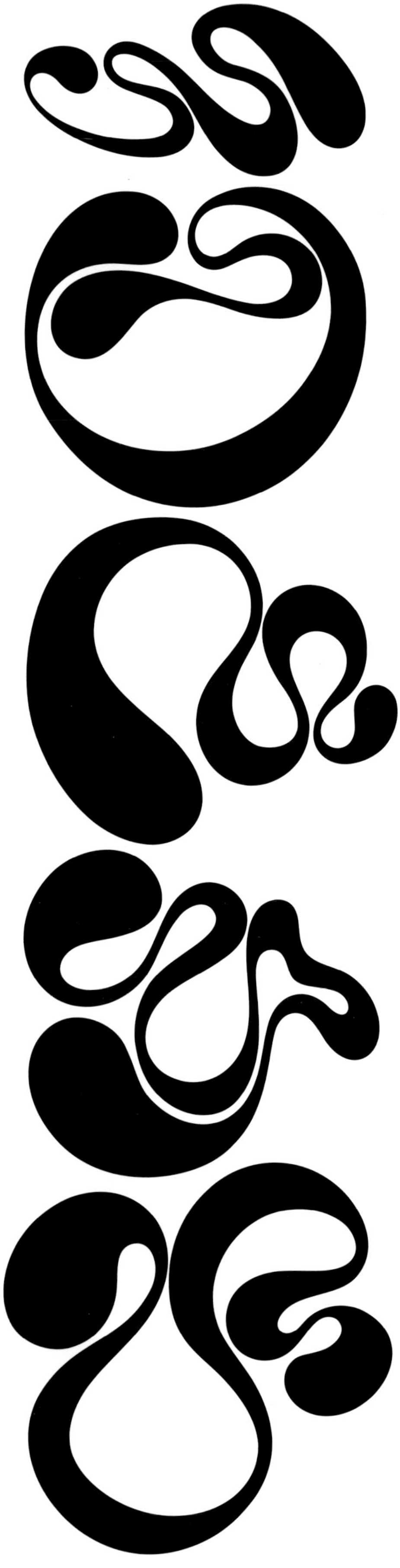

I HAVE NOT LOVED (ENOUGH OR WORKED)

unclaimed ideas

02

This book is the second title in The Art Gallery of Western Australia's new series, 'Unclaimed Ideas', and takes as its starting point the exhibition, *I have not loved (enough or worked)*. Both exhibition and book explore how our bodies and the subjective forces of love and desire are deeply enmeshed within the fantasy of the 'good life'.

The release of the book is timed to coincide with the show, which is the first major group exhibition from the Simon Lee Foundation Institute of Contemporary Asian Art presenting work by Hai-Hsin Huang, Daisuke Kosugi, Pixy Liao, Lin Zhipeng (aka No.223), Rinko Kawauchi, Sejin Kim, Lieko Shiga and Tao Hui. The exhibition brings together new and known voices working throughout Asia and the Asian diaspora, and gives AGWA's audiences the chance to view works by artists that have been rarely seen in Australia.

Featuring new writing, and with reprinted poetry on labour and love interspersed amongst the work of contemporary Asian artists, *I have not loved (enough or worked)* rethinks the value of work amidst the various crises which increasingly define this present moment. Contributors Mira Asriningtyas, Biljana Ciric, and Kelley Dong were invited to explore how the representation of 'love and labour' in contemporary art has evolved to reflect our current global social reality. Each writer pulls focus to feelings of anxiety and fear, loneliness and alienation, conflict and confusion, which we all endure on a daily basis. Each piece of art and text is distant yet familiar, such that experiencing the book evokes the pathos and yearning of navigating the world and its social complexity.

The Simon Lee Foundation Institute of Contemporary Asian Art is a major new creative and curatorial initiative at AGWA which will enrich and deepen the Gallery's connections with contemporary art practices and cultural thinking in Asia and its diaspora communities. We are exceptionally pleased to realise this visionary project in partnership with the Simon Lee Foundation, and to acknowledge the support and commitment of trustees, Orion Lee and Sarah D'Onofrio. This exhibition marks the first in a five-year partnership with Simon Lee Foundation to support contemporary Asian artists and thinkers.

We would like to thank Rachel Cieśla, Lead Creative, Simon Lee Foundation at AGWA, for her hard work as curator of the exhibition and editor of the book, and for her commitment to fulfilling the creative ambitions of the Institute. She has been supported by Bahar Sayed, Curatorial Assistant; Natalie Hewlett, Exhibitions Manager; Robert Cook, Senior Curator of Contemporary Art; and Aston Gibbs, Assistant Registrar. Appreciation goes to colleagues in the Conservation team: David Graves, Michael Houston, and Kate Woollett; the Marketing team: Sharyn Beor, Tanya Sticca and Penny Tassone; and the Exhibitions team: Todd Harrison, Dani Lye, Daniel Mead and Ako Roberts. Louella Hayes from the Development team was also instrumental in securing support for the exhibition. Thanks also to the many staff from across the gallery who have worked tirelessly to realise this project.

I have not loved (enough or worked) has been a collaborative project drawing upon the skills, expertise and creativity of many individuals from within our local and international community. In particular, we are grateful to Heesun Seo from Studio Hik for expertly crafting the exhibition's identity. Thanks also to Una X and Marco Dalle Fratte who designed the book.

Foreword

We would like to thank curator and writer Mira Asriningtyas for accepting our invitation to revisit her earlier text on unpaid labour in the knowledge economy through the lens of the global pandemic. Asriningtyas presents five case studies in the Jogja art scene which reconsider how value is assigned in artistic production. We are grateful to curator Biljana Ciric for taking the time to speak with each artist about their work, and shaping those conversations into a series of intimate letters addressed to the artists and curator of the exhibition. Thanks too to writer, producer and filmmaker Kelley Dong whose insightful essay on Shunji Iwai's film *A Bride for Rip Van Winkle* explores the theme of performance as it relates to love and labour. Dong's text provides a cinematic mode for understanding many of the works in this exhibition, and recognising how the obligation to perform can become an obstacle which blocks our ability to love freely and truly. These three newly commissioned texts are presented alongside Lisa Robertson's poem, 'Face', published in her 2010 collection *R's Boat*, from which the title of this book is drawn.

We are grateful for the generous support of The Art Gallery of Western Australia Foundation which has made this book possible. The exhibition and publication has also been supported by the Australian Government through the Australia Council for the Arts, its arts funding and advisory body, as well as the Australia-Japan Foundation and the Australia-Korea Foundation of the Department of Foreign Affairs and Trade.

Finally, we would like to express our deep gratitude and appreciation to the artists Hai-Hsin Huang, Daisuke Kosugi, Pixy Liao, Lin Zhipeng (aka No.223), Rinko Kawauchi and Nao Amino, Sejin Kim, Lieko Shiga, and Tao Hui. Each has created powerful works that delight, inspire and challenge us, and it has been our great pleasure to work with them on this project.

Colin Walker
Director,
The Art Gallery of
Western Australia

Orion Lee
Trustee, Simon
Lee Foundation

Kedela wer kalyakoorl ngalak Whadjuk boodjak yak.

The Art Gallery of Western Australia acknowledges the traditional custodians of the lands on which we work, the Whadjuk Noongar people in Boorloo, Perth.
We honour and pay respect to community Elders and to their ancestors who survived and cared for this Country. The Gallery recognises that sovereignty was never ceded.

A study in Labour and Love

Rachel Cieśla

A study in labour and love.

Recognise your failures.

You only love that which you can lose so loosen your grip, let her slip through your fingers.

Past loves cannot be returned to the here and now.

We experience multiple separations.

All caretaking is detachable from and attachable to.

We have each other, we take from each other.

Love is mutual loss.

Our personal relationships have always informed our labour networks.

You keep searching for a structural replacement to love, become a professional lover or quit economising your empathy.

Love is the most effective means of creating time and energy.

There is no joy to be found in fulfilment, only in recognition.

You cannot comprehend compassion without separation.

Never pay your debts.

Always be prepared to suddenly depart. Your lover will wait forever.

The body can't expand, art can't feel, and people can't express a range of self.

All bodies are flattened.

All we have are bodies and confirmation biases in collision.

All positions are essentialised.

All bodies are faceless.

Yoko Ono's *Cut Piece*, 1964, is a body with a face, a pain recognisable.

If we can expand our bodies to recognise a range of selves then how can we occupy or explore new territory outside ourselves? What ground will be gained? Or more so, what liberties have we surrendered in service of ourselves?

Call it what you will.

You can try to hold the centre or you can try to hyper-normalise the violence.

See inflammatory rhetoric and whipping up of false division.

Or remove all complexity and build a 'fake world'.

If we are all set on refusal, if we can be multiple – and not all of us can, nor should – then we must extend this same refusal to others.

I know you have not loved
(enough or worked).

It is an extractive logic that ties productivity to guilt. As if it is the creator's intention to problematise 'the social' as something that can be understood from within but only sensed from the outside.

Can we not apply this same understanding to our social interactions? Might we knowingly misunderstand in order to bring into being other kinds of emotions that are not necessarily connected to a secondary misinterpretation but instead reference the primary act?

I do not need to be responsible for the actions of my character because it truly is an age where everyone can be and is a performer.

Living together we haven't made
ourselves better.

We exchange glances but I divert my gaze for I was told that I cannot see.

I search for truth in a photograph but my eyes drift to a previous life I can no longer recall, for I don't recognise myself.

I want to go home.

On average are you better or worse than your grandparents?

My father says I'm being melodramatic but how should I face the future?

It wasn't how I imagined but sometimes work isn't all that important.

Much hope, no change.

I kid.

I'm not afraid, except for losing you.

I have not loved (enough or worked) – the intimacy of the title speaks to the individual, implying that you yourself have not done enough, or calling into question what you have done. It is an emotionally moralistic title which measures your personal and professional productivity in relation to feelings of guilt, shame, anger and despair and to matters of connection, care for others, and care for the self.

Love cannot be separated from work. In addressing love's relationship to labour – specifically the labour of love – knowing it is impossible to untangle love from work, and meaningless to suggest otherwise, I will not critique such labour as precarious or hidden. Nor will I suggest that work needs to be measured by compensation and utility or imply that it is wholly perpetuated by structures of power, as if such constructions are mutually exclusive, capable of containment and isolation. Instead, I want to reflect on how people hold themselves together and support each other is analogous to how nations, territories and regions construct and hold themselves together as a whole. To think, with Gregory Bateson, that a stick is a *pathway* instead of a boundary. And so it follows that there is no inside or outside; the everyday engagements between people, creatures, objects and ideas are co-constitutive. By acknowledging our distinction without treating ourselves as exceptional, can we create new possibilities for understanding and relating to each other? Or rather:

Can I exist without troubling to think?[1]

I have not loved (enough or worked) is a re-worked line from a poem by Lisa Robertson.[2] Like the poem itself, the work of each artist in this exhibition exists almost like an experiential, literary tale – one that opens out our experience of love and longing, loneliness and loss, and which contemplates how our understanding of these tangled, at times tortuous notions shape our relationships to the world as collectives, as pairs and as other social assemblies. The exhibition reveals how deeply enmeshed our bodies and the subjective forces of love and desire are within the fantasies of 'the good life'.

Bringing together works in video, photography, painting and sculpture by Hai-Hsin Huang, Rinko Kawauchi, Sejin Kim, Daisuke Kosugi, Pixy Liao, Lin Zhipeng (aka No.223), Lieko Shiga, and Tao Hui, the exhibition articulates the ways that people are fragile, finite. Their bodies, their subjectivities, are composed of pathways that need careful guarding and constant negotiation, just as feelings, memories and emotions pour out from each of us and complicate all kinds of encounters. It is this energetic dualism that defines our cultural, social and economic worlds and that we can reshape by uttering our intentions, asking questions, formulating ideas and committing to lofty abstractions.

By doing this, we might open up nasty wounds behind our hearts, and name the layers of love and loss that animate us, that reveal how our vulnerability is not a weakness but rather a place from which we compose new ways of being in the world and with each other, as friends, family, workmates and lovers ... or all at the same time. Such sentiments provide a platform to consider how these works were brought into being under an impulse to assert the complex existence of a temporal, multiply-inflected subject, in flux with the world around it. The project is

1. Jean-Jacques Rousseau: 'The ebb and flow of this water, its sound continuous but also marked by motions that ceaselessly patterned my ear and my eyes, supplemented my own emotion, calmed now by reverie, so that I felt in myself, so pleasurably and effortlessly, the sensation of existing without troubling to think'. See Lisa Robertson, *R's Boat* (Berkley and Los Angeles: University of California Press, 2010) vi.

2. Lisa Robertson, 'Face' in *R's Boat*, 2010, 1–13. See page 97.

an acknowledgment of the strange agency we fragile people have when we participate in that mobile re-shaping, together and alone.

Each artist in *I have not loved (enough or worked)* is an ardent observer of everyday life and the social structures that bind or separate us; or rather, of the structures that determine how people are to behave or ought to behave. In Kosugi's film *A False Weight*, 2019 we see the ways in which the protagonist Tadashi, a retired Japanese architect and bodybuilder, experiences his daily routines, and how these are poetically filtered through the various objects, surroundings, and people in his life. The work is an experimental portrait of the artist's father, Masanori Kosugi, who worked closely with Butoh dancer, Toru Iwashit, to choreograph a three-act narrative which gradually unfolds the experience of losing control of one's own body in a manner that is neither forced, strained or overly sentimental. What we experience is a man caught between his desire for personal freedom and acceptance of his declining body's new ways of being in and moving through the world. Ultimately, the title A *False Weight*, like that of this exhibition, is a fallacy. It is akin to the 'cruel optimism' which binds us to institutional structures, and which forces us to try and keep up with the good life that we seek to attain or maintain.[3] As Kosugi suggests, A *False Weight* carries a moral sensibility which allows him to understand his father's experience as well as demonstrate the marking of bodies as failed, unproductive and unwanted in accordance with the norm.[4] Speaking about *A False Weight*, curator Laura Herman asks:

3. Lauren Berlant, *Cruel Optimism* (Durham: Duke University Press, 2011).

4. Laura Herman and Daisuke Kosugi, 'The time of the body and the volcano: unpredictability and non-linearity' in *Daisuke Kosugi: A False Weight* (Paris and Bordeaux: Jeu de Paume and CAC, 2019), 24.

> Can architecture contribute to an alternative future for disabled bodies, or should our attitude to space and time be more inclusive of human unpredictability, the seismic shifts of the body? Perhaps it is more valuable to create architectures of community and affinity rather than dependency, necessitating an approach that constitutes an apprehension of self and other, of the affinities that are shaped, or not, within spatial settings.[5]

5. Ibid, 19.

Architecture has a stubbornness which can bind and fix our feet in place. This rigidity produces an idealised built environment and accompanying set of social structures that solidify their power by making the standardised body rely on certainty as a means of containing the apprehension of difference. Frustration erupts when an attempt is made to move beyond or turn away from architectural qualities that do not hold the potential for change.

Such tensions are enticingly revealed in Kosugi's accompanying sculptural works, *To hold on hold*, 2019 and *Recliner LC4*, 2019. Held together under tension, the bamboo structure of *To hold on hold* emulates the ambiguity of the human body. Its stable yet seemingly fragile spatial form disrupts the notion of a structural support as fixed, firm and upright. Similarly, *Recliner LC4* reinterprets Charlotte Perriand and *Le Corbusier's LC/4 Chaise Lounge*, 1928, by replacing the iconic tubular industrial steel with bamboo. A piece of furniture designed for the resting body of an impersonal, anonymous user, *LC/4 Chaise Lounge* emphasised the form, functionality, and force of twentieth century technological progress. As Herman notes, Kosugi's bamboo sculptures acknowledge contemporary design's concern for the creation

6. Ibid.

of safe, accessible places yet questions the notion of a universal, unchanging body for whom the chaise lounge is built.[6] In doing so, he makes us consider how not only objects but people and environments function (or fail to) as props and prosthetics. This flows back into the experience of love and longing, of caring for people and being separated from others – all the moments of connection and misconnection which keep our bodies under tension.

We can find a different sequence of generative tensions in the photobooks of Kawauchi. In *Cui Cui*, 2005, the space and pace of images is carefully determined by the artist – the photographs speed up, slow down, repeat and softly pause before bursting back out, creating an open dialogue which unfolds the larger themes of human existence. It is an element of her practice that questions the notion of borders – between birth and death, between one room and the next – to show there is no clear separation. Each photograph in *Cui Cui* is a memory of Kawauchi's family and hometown, which she had been shooting for 13 years. By capturing scenes of holidays, family gatherings, ageing and pregnancy alongside references to passages and crossings in the form of windows, doorways, streets and hallways, Kawauchi refers to the circularity of life, the movement of people, and the dynamic nature of memory.

We create such deceitful images and sublime renditions to service our human grief. Our need to reconcile the past and make bearable the present fuels the making of art. We know such production is but a dream for a better future, an attempt to heal what's gone and what's past help. As if we 'humans could defeat nature', as the broadcaster says in one of the nine videos that comprise Tao Hui's work *Hello, Finale!* 2017, 'Humanity is created by nature. What nature wants to take back it will take back.' Each performance, scripted in Japanese and filmed in Kyoto, is composed by the artist as a one-way dialogue spoken over the phone by an on-screen protagonist to an unknown recipient. The effect is distant yet familiar as we are held in the warmly nostalgic embrace of channel surfing and long-distance phone calls that represent all of us living things – whether aspiring actors now seeking to become professional housewives, husbands who know their relationships are beyond repair, anxious school children wanting to go home, or concerned mothers who think that work isn't all that important – navigating this world and its social complexity by performing ourselves better. All of us filled with pathos and yearning as we seek out connections with other living things. All of us anxiously flipping through the channels trying to find our true selves. All of us making that final phone call in a desperate attempt to move forward with our lives. All of us finding the courage to face the future.

The photographs of Shiga also carry with them fundamental questions about life and how to express oneself. In her series *Blind Date*, Shiga spent one week photographing around 100 couples riding motorbikes in Bangkok during the summer of 2009. For Shiga, the camera was the perfect tool for capturing the intimate distance needed to swap glances with a stranger. This act of shared looking revealed to her the insatiable desires which form the richness of human existence. Speaking on this body of work, Shiga says:

How much does the eye control us? I was told that I cannot see.

Does the reason for this relate to a previous life that I can no longer recall?

I wanted to know the truth, so I attended university and learned about many religions around the world.

Many, many things were said about life and death, but I felt uncomfortable about all of them.

They didn't quite match how I am.

We all endure feelings of alienation, conflict and confusion on a daily basis. These emotions are crisply pulled into focus in Kim's video *Urban Hermit*, 2016, in which a female cleaner slowly moves through a modern art museum. As we follow her on this journey, we encounter other museum workers – cleaners, security guards, and invigilators – all perfectly positioned within this highly controlled, pristine gallery environment. The video's two-screen configuration mirrors the linear arrangement of the museum's space, containing, minimising and isolating each worker in this larger structure. Alternating between footage of actual museum workers and the actors who play them, *Urban Hermit* presents itself as a series of atomised existential moments within a totalising whole.

Like Kim, Huang depicts the tension that exists between the harshness of reality and the idealised versions of life that we construct from the everyday. Huang's loose painterly approach to rendering people is honest and genuine, while at the same time highly performative and humorous. Painted in Taipei during the height of the Covid-19 pandemic in 2021, this new series of paintings describe the suffocating social experience of living with the virus. The obvious disconnect between the people and their environment – a man dives into a luxurious pool as fires rage around him, a choir performs amongst desert dunes, and figure skaters twirl under a hot pink sky – suggestive of our desire to escape an anxious existence that is unhinged from reality.

While Huang paints her 'inner landscapes' to create space for new ways of holding ourselves together, Liao sets up situations for herself and her boyfriend Moro to playfully perform and challenge gender roles through photography. In her ongoing project, *Experimental Relationship* (2007–), Liao often portrays herself in a dominant role and her boyfriend in a more submissive position, thus breaking the predominant relationship model and experimenting with new modes of being together.

Thinking about the messiness of human relationships, I realise why 223 composes the world through bodies. A photographed body is a temporary sculpture containing two forms of work: one that permanently arrests a mutable body in space and time, and another that cannot be held or replicated for it takes place as you click the shutter. The photograph unapologetically says, I can't forget you. It shows you that relationships will continue even as they change. Your friends will grow old, their homes might shift from Beijing to Paris, and some lovers may depart while others choose to stay. In 223's photographs we see bodies immersed in milky waters or decisively slumped against the wall. These are bodies that are not explicitly working but neither are they at rest. The fuzz of film and the fizz of flesh in these photographs draws us near, bringing us ever closer to that moment of irreplicable release and unencumbered joy. 223 reminds me that we carry love with us. And so it follows that we are always at work. We can never love enough or work enough. But know there is always enough love.

Rachel Cieśla

Rachel Cieśla is the Lead Creative for the Simon Lee Foundation Institute of Contemporary Asian Art at The Art Gallery of Western Australia, Boorloo/Perth.

Sugar, Spice, and Everything Nice:

A Proposal of Possibilities in Five Case Studies

Mira Asriningtyas

The art field is a space for wild contradiction and phenomenal exploitation. It is a place of power mongering, speculation, financial engineering, and massive and crooked manipulation. But it is also a site for commonality, movement, energy, and desire.[1]

1. Hito Steyerl, 'Politics of Art: Contemporary Art and the Transition to Post-Democracy', *Are You Working Too Much? Post-Fordism, Precarity, and The Labor of Art.* (Berlin: Sternberg, 2011) 37.

In mid-2017, I wrote a short essay on the topic of unpaid cognitive labor in the knowledge economy. Titled 'Sugar, Spice, and Everything Nice: A Proposal for Possibilities and Disobedience', the essay opened with an anecdote about spontaneously offering to share a piece of sweet giant stroopwafel with a friend and being asked 'Why?'. The calculative weight of the question over such a mundane act, triggered my consideration of how different cultural upbringings might shape a system of values that is socially determined as opposed to individually defined through capitalist structures. A love language for one could be a fear of debt for the other. One's naive thoughtless act could be contradictory to the internalised gift economy, permeating into the intimacy of sharing snacks with friends. Both points of view are no less true. One way of doing is just an alternative means of understanding the other. It didn't take long for me to regret writing this anecdote in such a petty way – a perceived failure on my part to probe its significance.

In this new text I intend to explore the complexity and specificity of value as critical to the shaping of society. Five years after the original essay, many things have changed while much has stayed the same. Navigating back and forth from the original piece to five case studies in Indonesia, this essay records the amplified precarity resulting from the global pandemic.

At the time of writing the original essay, I proposed a strike in the art world, addressing the question of 'how to say no to unpaid cognitive labor in the knowledge economy'. Back then, I thought:

If there were ever to be a strike upon unpaid cognitive labor in the art scene on my side of the world, nothing will ever be done. No more cultural production. No more civic movement. No more grassroots initiatives. No more contemporary art scene.

By 'my side of the world', I was specifically referring to case studies on cognitive labour within the context of the Jogja art scene. It is important to start by acknowledging Jogja as the site of my research, to recognise how value is understood within this context and how it shapes the social fabric of this city. For this purpose, I refer to curator Rizky Zaelani's understanding of 'criterion' and 'language' as interconnecting components.[2] Even if some values are untranslatable, the opacity and encounter between the non-Western apparatus of knowledge and the context for which this essay is written (in English, for an exhibition taking place in Australia) could be perceived as a site for instigation. In the end, the ephemeral concept of value as explained

2. Zaelani, Rizky. 'Interpellation: Notes on a Common Language of Comparison in International Art Events', Exhibition Catalogue for *Interpellation, CP Biennale* (Jakarta: CP Foundation, 2003), 13 June 2017.

through the following case studies might not be a totally foreign idea after all, when viewed from different sides of the world.

Instead of answering the question of how to say no to unpaid labour, in my earlier essay I tried to explore the possibility of an alternative value system outside of capitalism. Such a proposal does not necessarily mean that a cultural worker does not need to be paid. Whenever there is a means of monetary support, it is only fair to provide a decent wage for cultural workers. Rather, this essay supports seeking replacements to fiscal value within the economic equation and asking in what situations this scenario is valid. Possibilities present themselves in various forms: a generous structure of sharing knowledge and resources; an informal economy that involves giving and self-sufficiency, common goals and belief, care and reciprocity, a sense of belonging and freedom; a civic movement born out of necessity, friendship, kinship; and probably – love.

Case Study 1:

Stay Small or Rent a Haunted House!

Even with a relatively young public funding system for the arts in Indonesia, which has only recently begun to bloom, there is a robust art scene in every city with no shortage of contemporary art institutions and informal cultural infrastructures. The Indonesian artworld is notorious for its precarious public infrastructure. It is a sector that is largely self-organised with little reliance on formal infrastructure or public funding. It is not unusual for an art institution to be artist-run, self-funded and kept alive through the in-kind support of networks and friends. One of the most significant artist-run spaces is Cemeti (now 'Cemeti Institute for Art and Society'). Founded in 1988 in the living room of Mella Jaarsma and Nindityo Adipurnomo, Cemeti has significantly shaped the Indonesian contemporary art scene by promoting internationalisation during a period of political instability. It is now an established institution, but during the New Order Regime the idea of shifting private spaces into exhibition spaces was considered a political act against the government's control and censorship of art through state-initiated art and cultural institutions. Most of the public institutions that were built during Suharto's New Order represented the government's view of an ideal art activity, both as an event and in the way an artist chose to express their ideology through their work. To remain free from censorship and independent of the government's cultural agenda, contemporary art spaces like Cemeti needed to be self-funded and self-organised.

After the end of Suharto's dictatorship in 1998, censorship ceased, making it easier to create civil movements and new cultural initiatives. The fall of Ex-President Suharto and his regime encouraged many artists to open art spaces and establish their own initiatives in many Indonesian cities. Groups of young artists started renting residential houses, running them as (semi)public spaces where they could hang out with friends, make and show work, do gigs and organise projects. Each space had its own focus, ways of working and means of surviving. The result was dynamic and perpetually changing as new spaces easily popped-up and died. As most of these art initiatives were short lived, they tended to trigger each other and create a snowball effect which shaped the future of the Indonesian art scene. Between the acceleration of life and death of an 'alternative' space, what remained was a critical engagement with infrastructural development by the artists who flourished in its place. As a site of ideas, a physical space can be gone, but the idea of the space lives on within the person and the collective memory.

Not all art spaces die for economic reasons. But for those of us who live longer within this sphere of precarity, strategising economically happens on a day-to-day basis: the founder works a second job and treats the art space as their 'love child'; to afford the space, some decide to rent a haunted house as a cheaper alternative, others decide to stay small. To be small means to remain autonomous and free from the constraints of a bigger agenda. Being small also allows the art initiative to stay fluid, flexible, and open to collaboration. It is also less economically demanding. The strategy of staying small has also been applied by older independent art spaces, including Kedai Kebun Forum (KKF) in Yogyakarta. For more than 25 years, KKF has been holding an important position in the Indonesian art scene, yet it insists on making the political decision to remain 'small'. To be strategically small requires arriving at a position to say no to the opportunity and temptation to grow large. To stay small can then be seen as a deliberate refusal to be swallowed by the capitalist system.

I see the decision to stay small as the closest thing to a strike against the capitalist system in the art world. In Reinaart Vanhoe's book, *Also Space, From Hot to Something Else*, he notes two faciliatory structures that allow Indonesian art spaces to survive:

1. Supportive structures: the practical and theoretical support of each other's collective or individual artistic goals; and
2. Generous structures: the open-minded sharing of knowledge that offers an alternative to a calculating world.[3]

Such structures are possible partly due to Indonesian customs and the social concepts of gotong royong (mutual cooperation) as a form of collective support, and nongkrong (hanging out) as an informal process of knowledge transfer.

3. Reinaart Vanhoe, *Also-Space, From Hot to Something Else: How Indonesian Art Initiatives Have Reinvented Networking* (Eindhoven: Onomatopee, 2016), 33.

Case Study 2:

How To Do Everything When You've Got Nothing

When I consider facilitatory structures other than the two identified by Vanhoe, I recognise that the general resourcefulness and make-do mentality of Indonesians allows people to work with what they have and cross-subsidise projects to be able to do more with less. Perhaps Indonesians are living in the future? For, according to Buckminster Fuller's vision of ephemeralisation, in the future one can do more and more with less and less until eventually one can do everything with nothing.[4] Jokes aside, how does everything get done with nothing? Let's take two festivals as case studies: first, Binal Experimental Arts 1992 and second, the festival Untuk Seorang Lelaki yang Demikian Mencintai Hujan in 2021.

4. Richard Buckminster Fuller, *Nine Chains to the Moon* (New York: Anchor Books, 1973) 252–59.

Historically, the pioneering biennale in Jogja started as a government initiative which aimed to form the cultural identity of the nation. Operating within this narrow national vision and mission, the biennale was limited to painting as an art form, and was somewhat loaded with top-down direction that prevented artists from creating an immediate response to the current socio-political situation in Indonesia. That was until a counter-festival, Binal Experimental Arts 1992, was created by young artists as a form of protest to the establishment. The nine-day artist-led counter-festival featured multiple art forms ranging from installation to performance. The name 'Binal' (translated as untamed/wild/disobedient) is another form of pronunciation for 'biennale'. Project funding barely existed so everything was done with almost nothing. Artists and the community worked together to reclaim public spaces. They opened up their studios as makeshift galleries; publications and invitations were shared through networks of friends; and others donated their time and energy to the event. In order to overthrow authority and change the top-down repression of the State, the citizens needed to take over the official biennale platform and perform the role and function of government. This newly created network of small grassroot movements manifested into a city-wide art festival which slowly came to power – a crawling coup d'état. Binal received more publicity and spotlight than the original biennale and, while maintaining freedom of expression and experimentation, soon replaced it as the city's bottom-up biennale platform which later became the Jogja Biennale that we recognise today.

Sharing a common goal and an accessible cultural vision are two elements that can trigger a movement amongst people and ignite a voluntary state of being. In such situations, the human resources of the art scene will autonomously work for a common cause and not for reputational or economic gain. Starting from this point of view, networks and friendships cannot merely be seen as a dirty or fragile reputational economic move. Instead, it becomes a safety net through which to strengthen the movement and reach a common goal. Hospitality and trust become crucial modes of exchange when building a stronger and more tolerant society; while the presence of a generous structure allows reciprocal learning processes to happen at the grassroots level. Within this framework art is no longer art, but what we can achieve with it.

I recently experienced a similar burst of energy in commonality through my involvement with a small festival, Untuk Seorang Lelaki yang Demikian Mencintai Hujan (loosely translated as 'For a Man Who Fell for the Rain'). At the end of 2021, our community lost Gunawan Maryanto, a beloved poet, artist, theater icon and a good friend to many. A generous, genuinely supportive, and caring person, he was also humble, inclusive, and egalitarian. So much so that, to process our collective loss and grief, we held a festival to commemorate the 100th day of his passing, embodying the same spirit and qualities that he shared in his lifetime. Everybody chipped in, sparkles burst into fireworks, artists and friends flew to Jogja (even from Bali, Jakarta, Melbourne and New York) to volunteer and celebrate his life, and resources were suddenly abundant. I remember thinking how easy it was to throw a festival for a generous person. Multiple art spaces opened their doors for exhibitions, others provided a stage for an all-night-long music concert; musicians lined up to perform their tribute; videographers and live streaming providers recorded the festivities so that people all over the world could join in; art handlers provided their service for the full duration of the festival, and exhibition equipment was borrowed from multiple institutions. As part of the festival's main team, I rediscovered the poetics in human resourcefulness and connection that had felt distant during the global pandemic. Friends referred to the process as 'festival *unitalicise*'. Sambatan originates from the Javanese word *unitalicise*, meaning to lament or ask for help. Culturally, sambatan refers to a specific act of gotong royong – to help others who are in need of manpower and neighbours' assistance. A lot of the resources required for the festival were acquired by asking clearly for exactly what was needed. In the process, a lot of care was put into the resources and people who helped with the sambatan: empathy and tolerance were used to assess labour conditions, the duration of the show was shortened to limit our usage of the borrowed projector, and the different hosts of each smaller event provided lunch for everyone involved. In less than three months, another chain of movements and smaller events turned into a month-long festival in Jogja and beyond. What started from grief and loss turned into movement and energy.

In her essay, *Wok the Rock & Co.: Making Sense of Friendship in Yogyakarta's Art Scene*, researcher and writer Nuraini Juliastuti noted, 'When an activity is done in the spirit of gotong royong, labour is valued as fleeting, abundant, and free.'[5] In the context of the Indonesian art scene, having an awareness that we are in the same situation and that art can be a vehicle for social change makes such kinds of voluntary action easily available – people and their kinship become a crucial resource. When doing the act of gotong royong, people provide collective support without expecting a favour in return. Yet, to receive an act of gotong royong means being open to the expectation that you will be ready when it is your turn to do the work. Even if people do not expect a favour in return, the debt is to the community itself. There is never a binding contract, however the sense of responsibility is highly personal and often fragile. At the same time, it creates a site of possibility and potential for long-term supportive structures to establish themselves in a continuous cycle.

5. Nuraini Juliastuti, 'Wok the Rock & Co.: Making Sense of Friendship in Yogyakarta's Art Scene,' *Discipline Journal* No.4 (December 2015): 1–20.

Case Study 3:

On Safety Nets and Kinship

Even without the pandemic, working in the arts is precarious. Never mind working in an art scene with no history of public financial support and a very young, bureaucratic platform for government funding. That is why the so-called 'alternative way' of doing things was crucial for artists and the Indonesian art scene to survive. But when the Covid-19 pandemic hit the planet, it was all about actual human survival. Everything that we knew was being questioned, our values were recalibrated, and the precarious structures which determined our lives were suddenly put on a pedestal with a spotlight on them. How do you make art when art does not seem to make sense? Could you possibly put the survival of an art space before your own? What good is art if you risk your own life?

Life was put on a major worldwide pause as we collectively tried to understand the virus. We were adapting to its presence and struggling for our survival; collective grief and despair hung in the air while we were all physically distancing ourselves from each other. The ground in Jogja was shaking as our close-knit art scene felt the loss of our usual practice of nongkrong. Multiple gigs within Indonesia and abroad were cancelled as the borders between nations remained closed, while project and exhibition opportunities were lost. This moment of crisis spurred us to question the system and rethink the urgencies of our times. For us, it is reassuring to be part of a close-knit community during moments of isolation as we re-learn how to be together as neighbours in a non-distanced society. But is it possible to imagine a collective movement without proximity? Can we hope to live more sustainably in the world after this great mutation?

Nongkrong, or a casual get-together to talk about nothing and everything at the same time, has been an important process in weaving the social fabric of the Jogja art scene. Artist and writer Sonja Dahl, explains in her essay:

> nongkrong as it is practiced among Jogja's artists, intellectuals and activists is actually a profoundly productive and creative practice that functions without overt regard to the capitalist model … more akin to 'non-productive time' – neither overtly goal-driven, nor unproductive in the capitalist sense. Rather than focusing on end-product productivity, nongkrong offers a holistic view of art as a long-term social process. It is a site of potential action, a social space that is all about the pleasures of sharing time with friends.[6]

6. Sonja Dahl, 'Nongkrong and Non-Productive Time in Yogyakarta's Contemporary Arts,' Parse Journal, 2017. 14 June 2017.

During this time, knowledge is transferred, a chance of collaboration opens, and the bond between people within the community strengthens. This mode of knowing and acquiring knowledge independently requires a generous structure: willingness to share thoughts and at the same time to give time and attention to other people's thoughts. Often it requires trust and attentiveness. Without the generosity of sharing knowledge and the attentiveness to receive new knowledge, the potential of nongkrong will degrade to a meaningless act performed out of habit or peer pressure. Yet, it opens up a space for possibility and, within the sphere of possibilities, changes can happen.

Confronted with our vulnerability and precarity in the whirlwind of the early pandemic, the art scene in Jogja put all artistic production aside and collectively created 'collaborative survival' strategies. For example, a temporary community group collected donations to provide oxygen tubes during the crisis; another collective formed an online promotional platform for artists to sell food and other products to survive. All over town solidarity platforms popped up for specific causes and needs. In general, artist collectives perform as an extended family, a function that is especially crucial during a time of crisis. Although they are resilient, artist collectives are decidedly fragile by nature so alternatives to the usual 'alternative' way of doing things need to be continuously reassessed and recalibrated – just like everything else post-pandemic.

One collective of artists using photography, MES56, was quick to respond to the situation. Even though MES56 has been running for 20 years on mostly ad hoc economies of friendship, the pandemic revealed the urgency of finding new ways to financially support its members. Multiple platforms of income-sharing have since been implemented on top of the artist-led solidarity movement. Early on, when the pandemic hit, MES56 initiated a 'mask for all' movement, allowing them to still be nongkrong for the purpose of making and distributing face masks. Later, upon realising that day-to-day life was getting harder for some, they initiated an open kitchen where people could donate food produce to be cooked in the collective kitchen. Everyone in need was welcome to eat there or take away the food. A similar initiative was created by KKF who turned their art space into a makeshift emergency kitchen that distributed hundreds of food boxes every day to the precariats and people on the street. The movements grew bigger and wider than the internal arts community in an attempt to collectively create both a safety net and a platform for sustainable collaborative life.

These examples of collaborative survival strategies are not unique to the Jogja art scene. Solidarity movements and multiple attempts to create collective safety nets were initiated throughout Indonesia at both a neighborhood and national scale. In general, the principle of collaborative survival means that an act of care is not necessarily a large donation. Rather, it can be as simple as making sure that nobody in your neighborhood is hungry or cold on a daily basis. The movement starts from small ripples in multiple places until a wave is formed. In such a close-knit society our precarious life and existential vulnerability is met with kinship and generosity.

Case Study 4:

On Generous Structures that Make the (Art) World Go Round!

Five years after being taken aback by the calculative weight of being asked 'Why?', ironically I found myself stepping into the shoes of the one asking the question. It happened before the opening ceremony of the third iteration of a site-specific project that I curated in my hometown Kaliurang, titled *900mdpl*.[7] A lady dressed in kebaya and batik with a matching scarf and red sandals came in with a jumbo jar of sweet hot tea. I did not remember ordering this, so I asked

7. 900mdpl is a biennial site-specific project in Kaliurang, Yogyakarta that proposes to create a growing socially-engaged archive of the village and to preserve the collective memories of the people. Kaliurang is an aging historical resort village seven kilometres away from the caldera of Mount Merapi, one of the most active volcanoes in Indonesia. See www.900mdpl.com.

our host ‘Why?’. The *900mdpl* project was created with close-to-zero funding and so I was overly conscious about additional costs. I was worried that I had mistakenly ordered an extra jumbo jar of hot tea. ‘No specific reason. It's just her thing to bring tea for everybody during a community gathering’, explained the host whose house became our office during the exhibition week. Apparently, the jumbo jar of tea was her way of supporting the event. Just like the host himself, who opened his door to our gathering for the duration of the exhibition.

Every day, a group of local painters and other exhibiting artists would voluntarily gather in the courtyard to attend the show and talk to anyone about their work in their own words. Our host made sure that we never ran out of fragrant crispy-fried bananas or boiled cassava from their garden, served with freshly ground chilli-garlic, to accompany the endless flow of conversation. The people who were nongkrong there changed every once in a while, and everybody was welcome. In the afternoon, when the weather got cold, a big bowl of steaming hot noodle soup would be ready on the table for anyone who needed the comfort of it. The next day, a neighbour showed up with a ripening banana from her own garden as a form of contribution and to make sure that we would never run out of the famous crispy-fried bananas. Not only was the exhibition free to visit, the audience could also enjoy fresh fruits, small snacks, and whatever else was brought in by the neighbours, and served on the table during their visit.

For the opening, a group of local musicians decided to chip in. Consisting of 25 people from the houses around the exhibition site, the group would gather twice a week to practice the syncretic Islamic prayer song in Javanese gamelan so that the audience of the exhibition had 'something to listen to' while looking at the art. When I asked whether it troubled them to do this, they protested my question, declaring the exhibition to be part of the community event – to not be a part of it would make them feel like they were not being involved. To give and to invite is to build their personal sense of ownership of the exhibition itself, but, even more so, it is a collective attempt to reclaim value from capital’s logic.

Later that day, a huge buffet arrived for everyone's brunch. We ordered one tumpeng only but the caterer threw in the buffet as a bonus to support the exhibition, and fed almost 75 people! The generosity of the neighbours and all the care being put into the exhibition made me realise that it is incorrect to say that the project had close-to-zero funding. All this time, rather than ‘making everything with nothing’, it was making everything with an abundance of support in the form of a ripening banana, a banquet lunch, a jumbo jar of tea, a bowl of noodle soup, or simply by being present. The project funding was presented as an informal economy that involved giving and self-sufficiency, care and reciprocity, kinship and a sense of belonging. I realised then that this third iteration of *900mdpl* did not work 'with' the community, nor did we 'engage' the community for a 'participatory' project. We are part of the community and we are all in this together.

Case Study 5:

Reason to Celebrate / Get Together / Being

You might realise, as we go through this stream of thoughts and case studies, that providing generous structures of care is never about taking a radical step into the unknown. According to Indonesian scholar Suka Hardjana, the tradition of gotong royong is more of a character than a tradition – instinct instead of essence, existing but not absolute, and always volatile.[8] Gotong royong as an act of volunteerism can be found in multiple forms across many different parts of the world because to help those in need is a universal human value.

As Reinaart Vanhoe maintains, it is possible to create an also-possible world[9] if we see ourselves as part of a network that can influence, encourage, and provide feedback that offers propositions and alternative possibilities of doing things. Such a proposition is better explained in the table below.

8. Suka Hardjana, 'Falsafah Sapu Lidi Membaca Kembali Manusia Indonesia: Defisit Individu Dalam Kerumunan Massa Politik Gotong Royong', presented at the Equator Symposium 2014, Graduate Program of Gadjah Mada University, Yogyakarta.

9. Vanhoe, Also-Space, 89.

10. Ibid.

From Hot...[10]		...to Something Else
Profit-driven, market-driven	networking	Benefit-driven, community-driven
Networking in order to increase one's visibility within the art scene	effort	Networking in order to learn and share knowledge
Individual careers	value	Working towards common goals
Effort to be seen; energy is focused on being represented, on being present and valuable, on being credited	visibility	Effort to engage with and relate to the context of everyday production; effort to give and receive
Internal community	reputation	Different communities Internal community

Table 1: From Hot to Something Else
Reinaart Vanhoe, *Also-Space, From Hot to Something Else: How Indonesian Art Initiatives Have Reinvented Networking* (Eindhoven: Onomatopee, 2016), 89.

On a more personal level, we are all familiar with this terrain. We know how it feels to work extra jobs to support our art practice, hoping to make the world a better place. We give up the idea of having a child or a house, or even the privilege of mobility, simply because we don't have enough time or money as art makes us constantly overworked or broke. But if you see the possibilities in collectivity, you will make use of what is available for the good of many people: for overthrowing corrupt governments, or to simply make your community more friendly, or your neighbours less suspicious of one another. And if you still need to remind yourself why you are doing what you are doing in the art world, here is the last desperate reason: love.

But what if the love dies a little?

When the pandemic made us question the impact of mobility on the art world, shedding light on overproduction while we were busy grieving and trying to survive, a few little things died a little: the joy and intimacy of being together without fear of contagion, reasons to celebrate, and a sense of purpose in art-making. Perhaps now we need to ask ourselves the calculative 'why'? Why do we keep on doing what we are doing and continuously recalibrate our values? Is it for a sense of belonging and purpose?

It is not surprising that the artworld quickly flocked to perennials once the borders between nations reopened. In togetherness, we allow ourselves joy. The pandemic reminded us to dwell in the lightness of a celebration in the presence of opportunity and we can now start to anchor ourselves differently in our practice. Looking back, those reasons (on top of love and generous support structures) gave a bolt of energy to events like 900mdpl, Festival Untuk Seorang Lelaki yang Demikian Mencintai Hujan, and all the bigger perennial events around the world. Once again, we need to have reasons to be together, to celebrate, and just to be. If we allow ourselves a little joy and a moment of recovery, perhaps we can slowly start a crawling coup d'etat against the precarious structure we are all in.

Mira Asriningtyas

Mira Asriningtyas works as an independent curator and writer in Yogyakarta, Indonesia. She has curated exhibitions and public programs for De Appel Art Center, Amsterdam; Stedelijk Museum, Amsterdam; Fondazione Sandretto Re Rebaudengo, Turin; KKF, Yogyakarta; International Studio and Curatorial Program, New York; and MAIIAM Contemporary Art Museum, Chiang Mai.

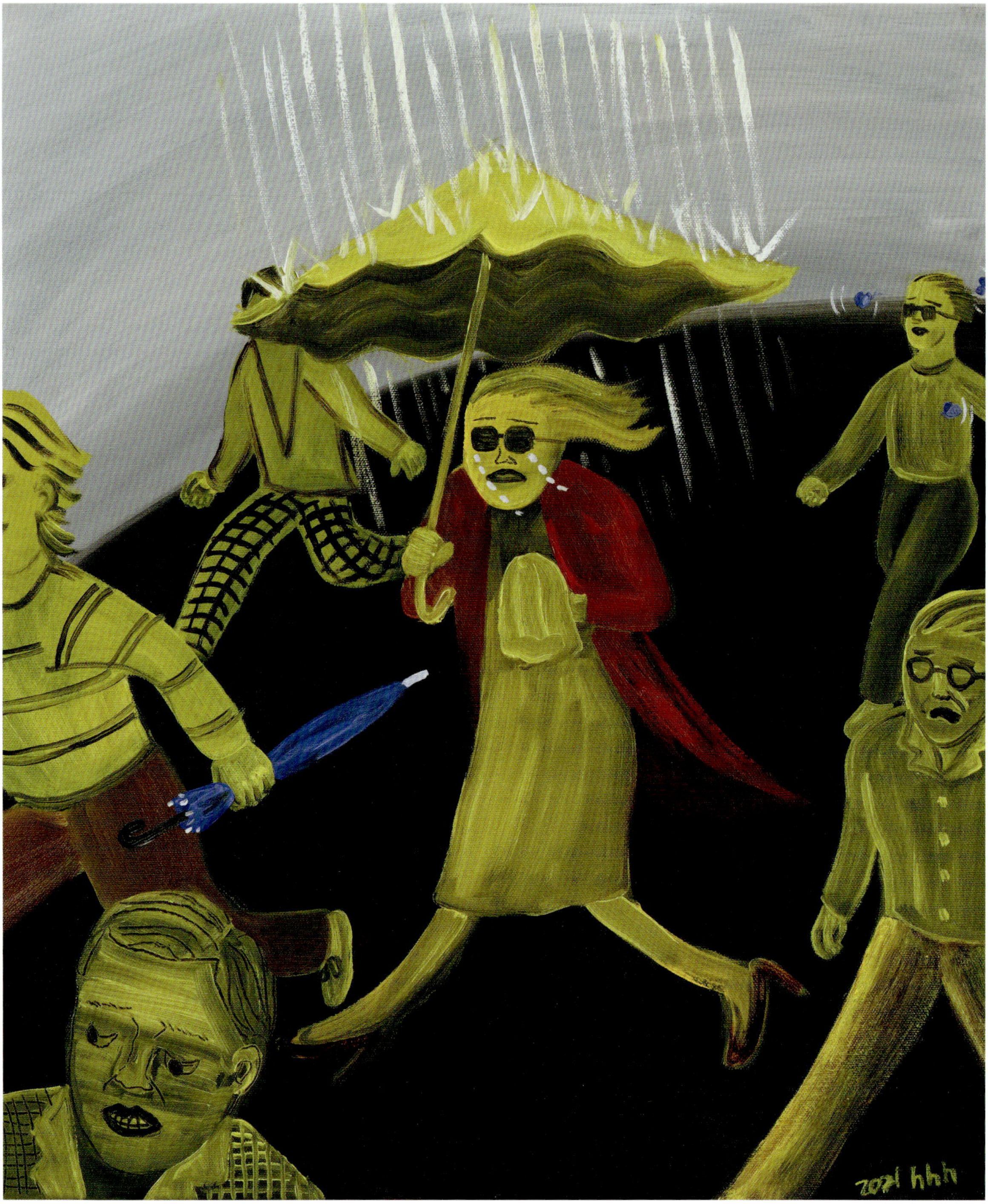

〔01〕

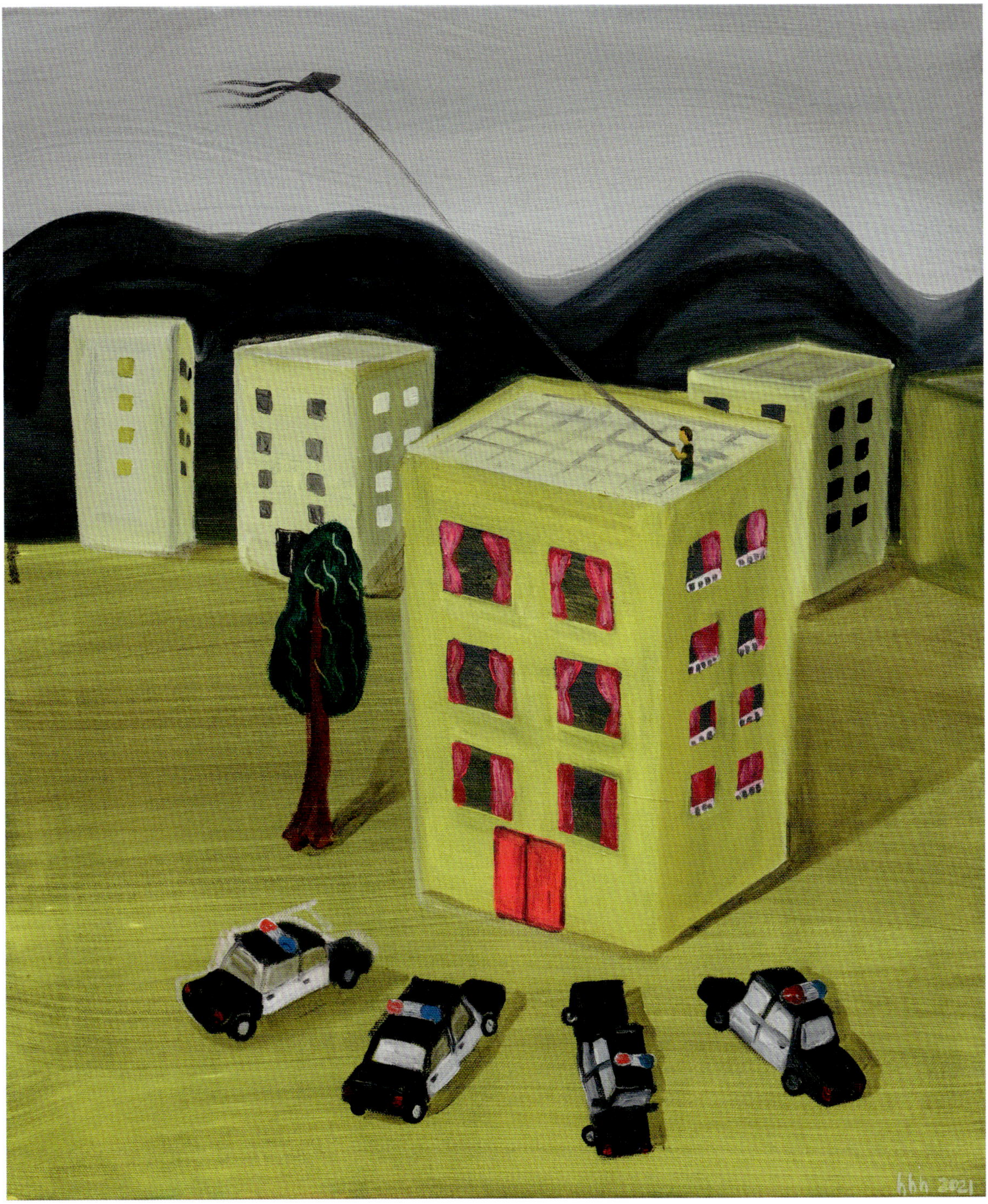

(02)

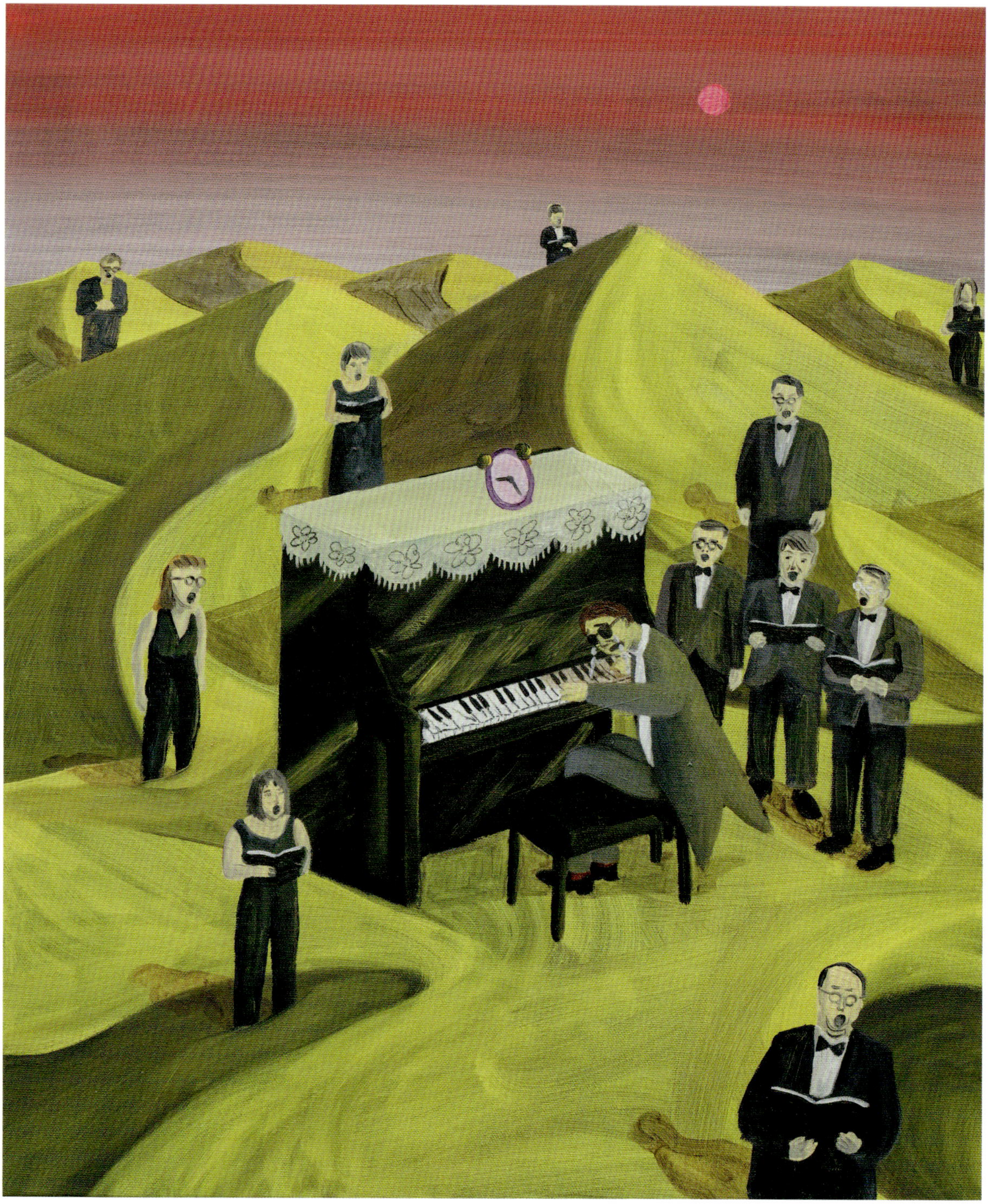

(03)

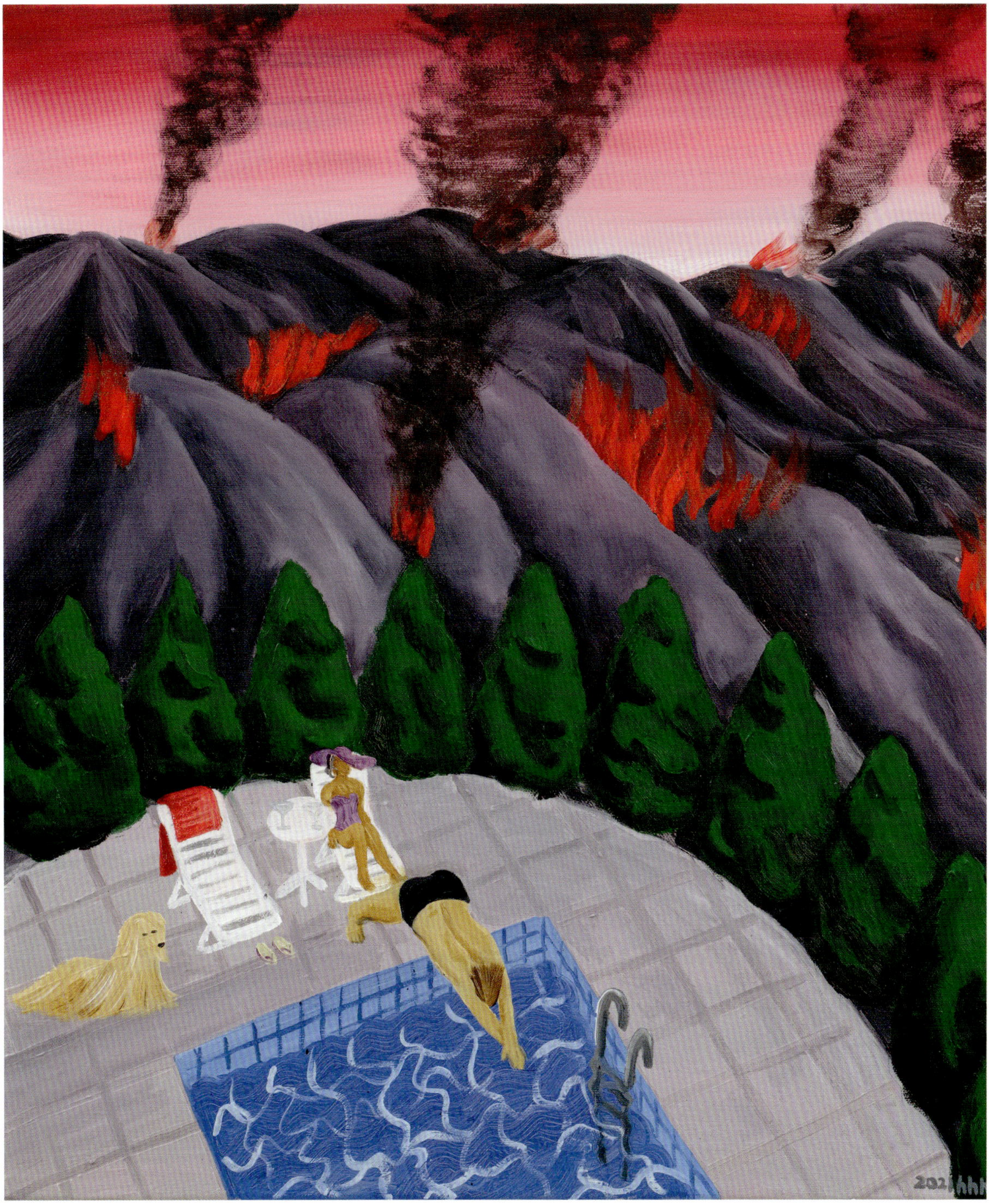

(04)

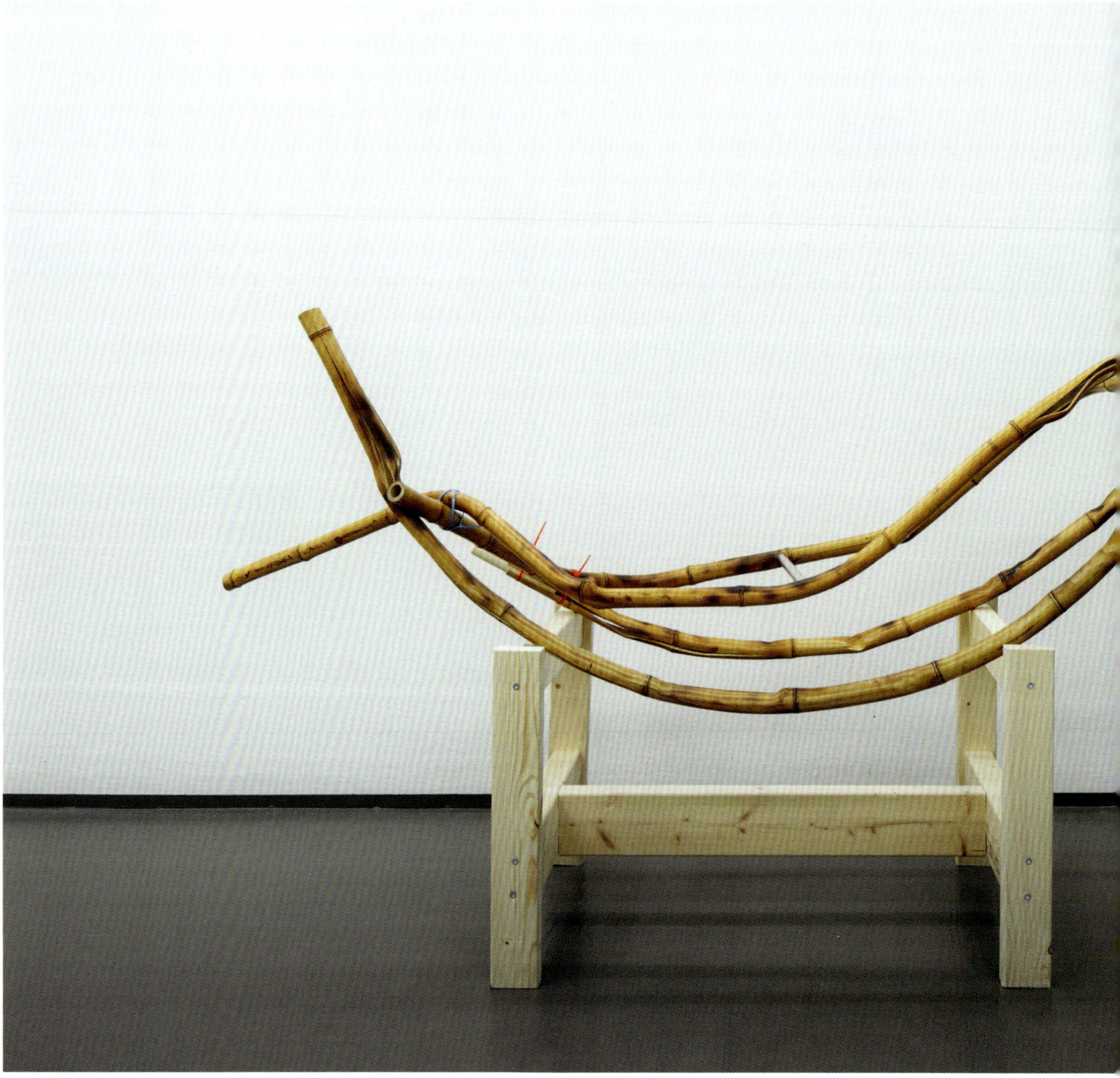

(05)

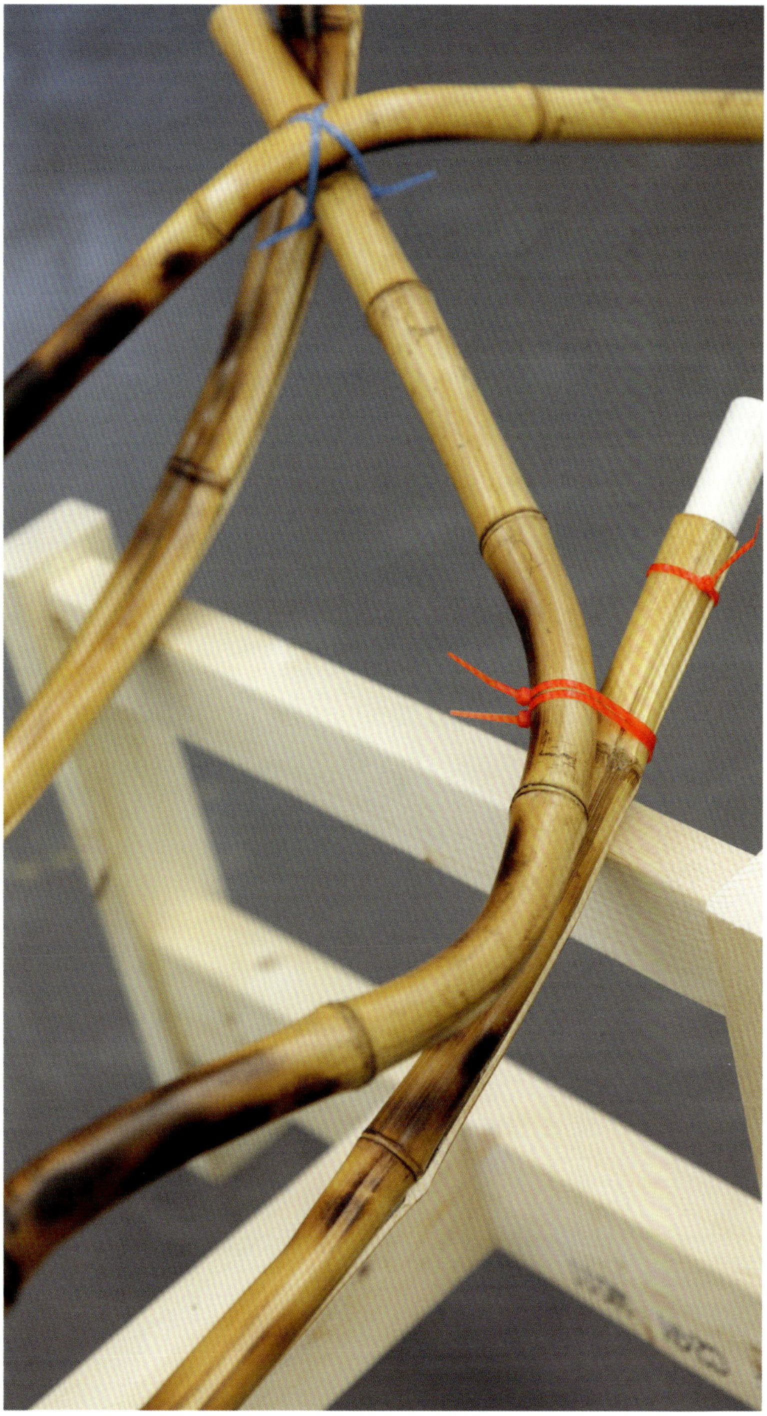

〔06〕

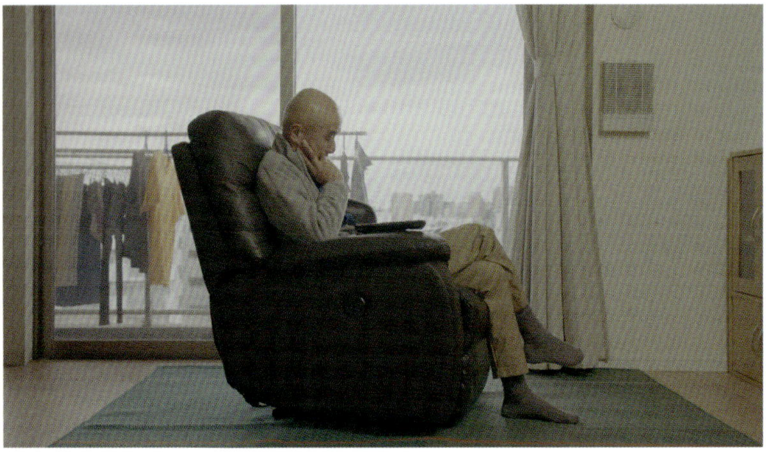

〔07〕

〔08〕

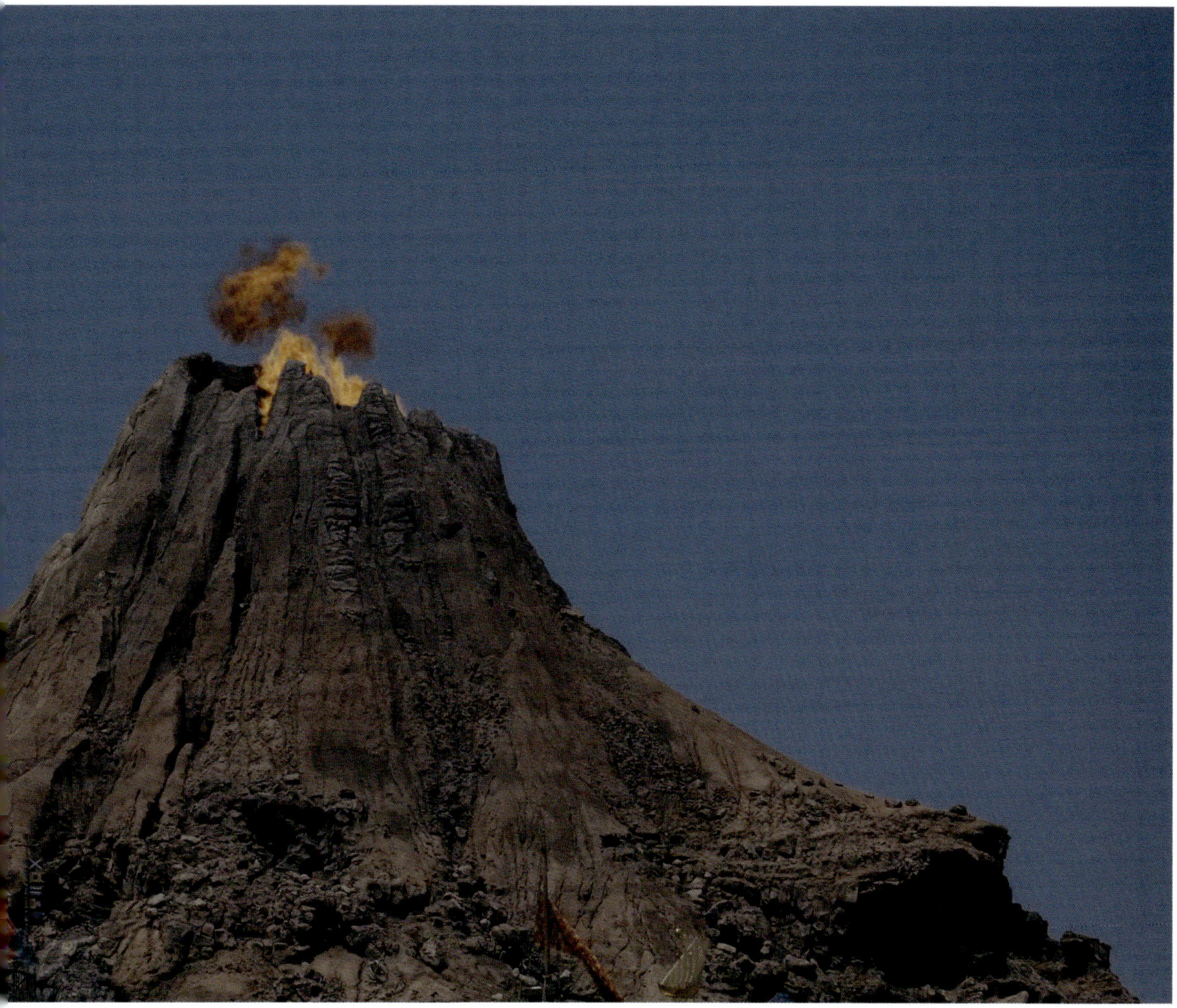

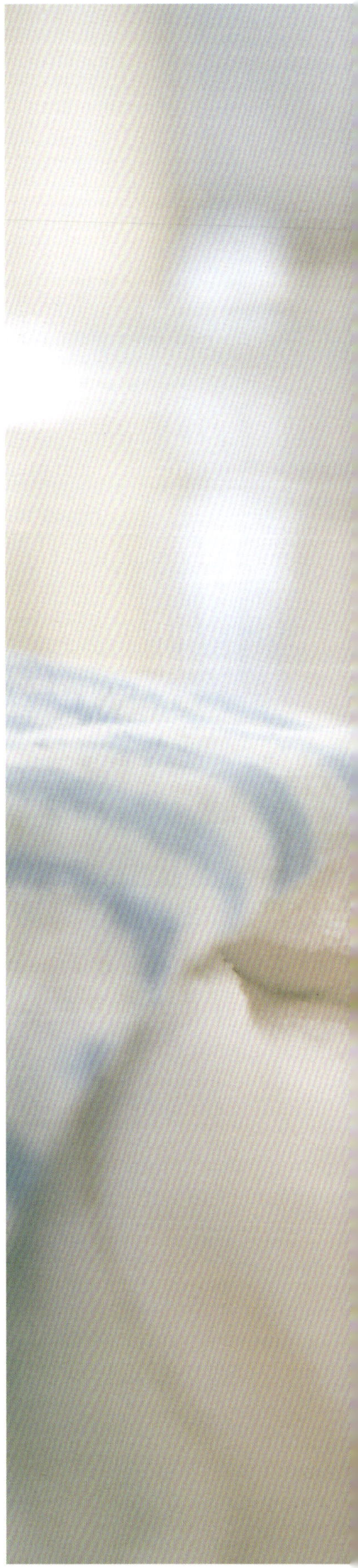

(09)

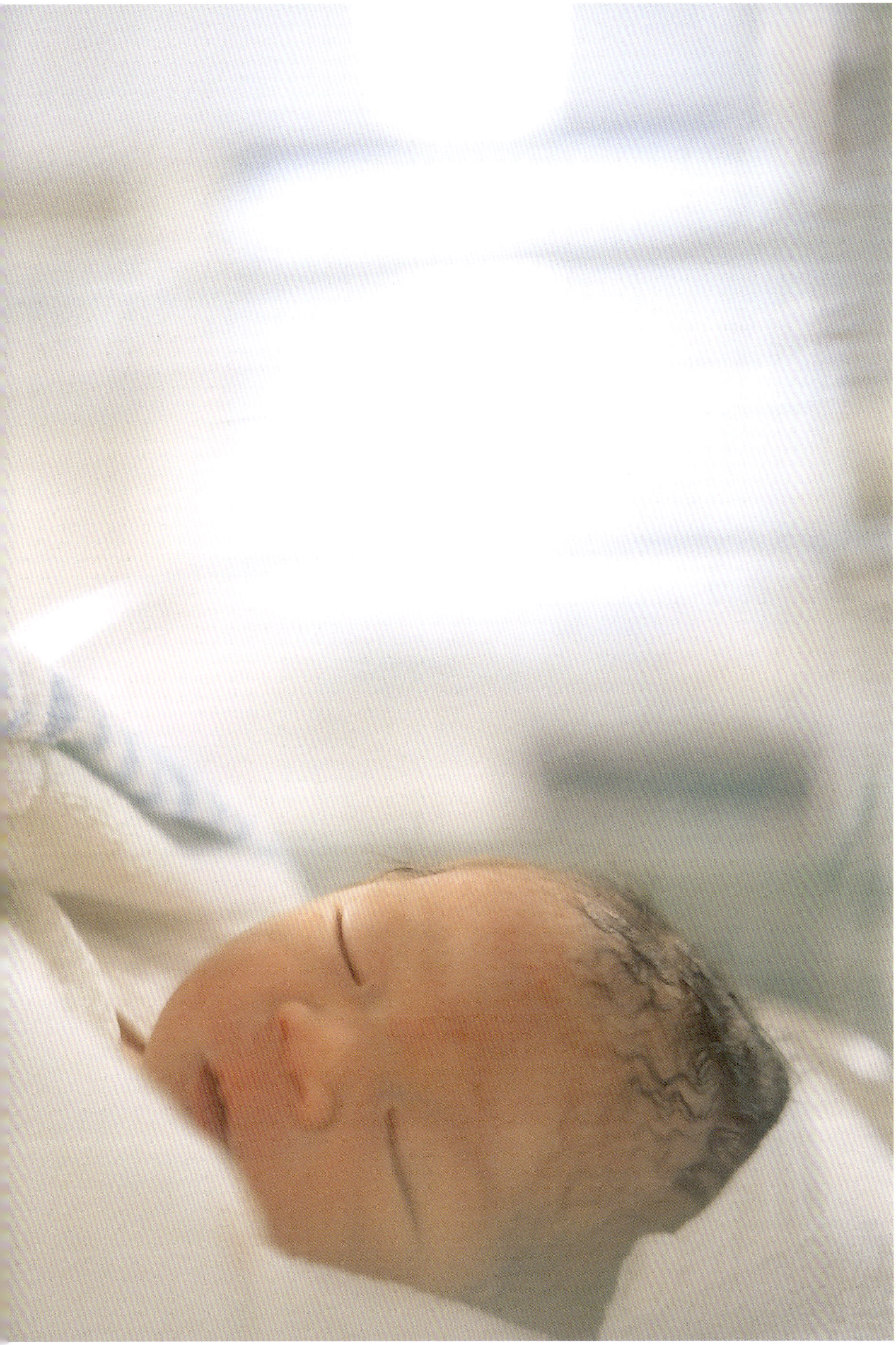

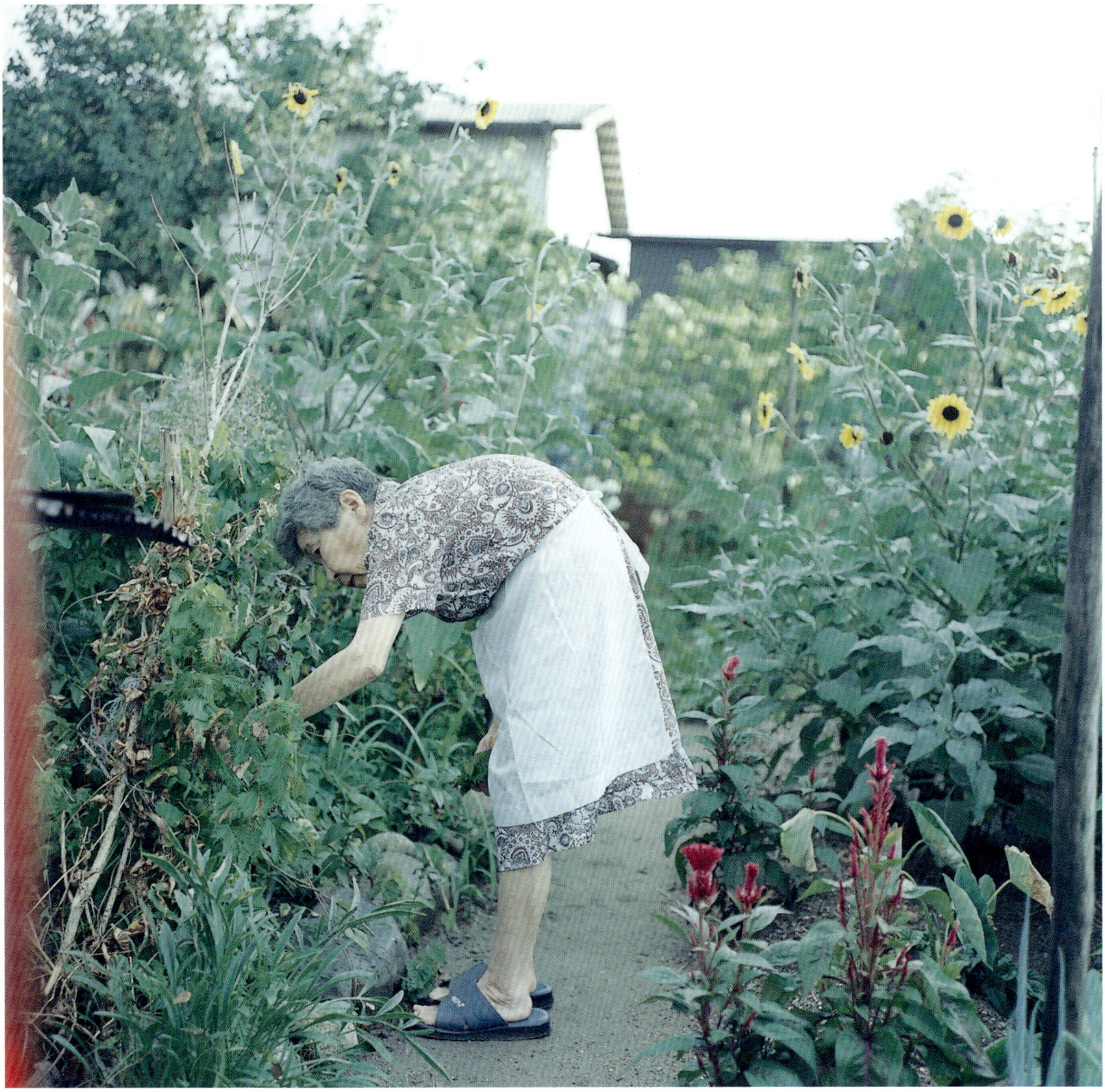

(10)

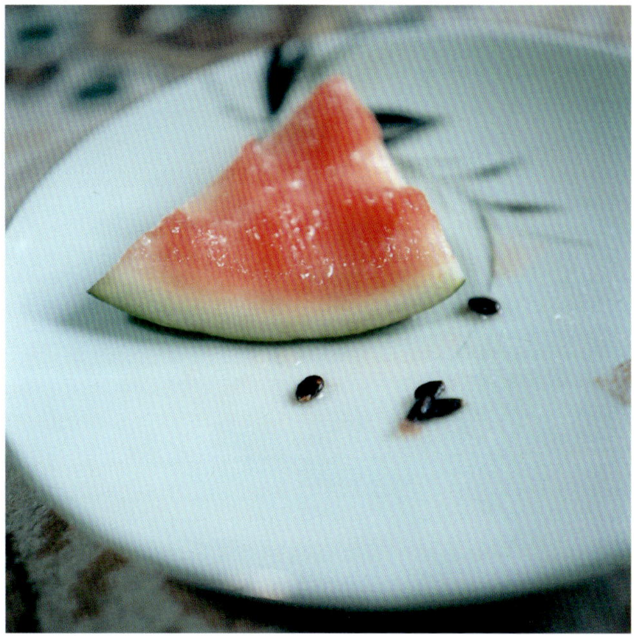

(11)

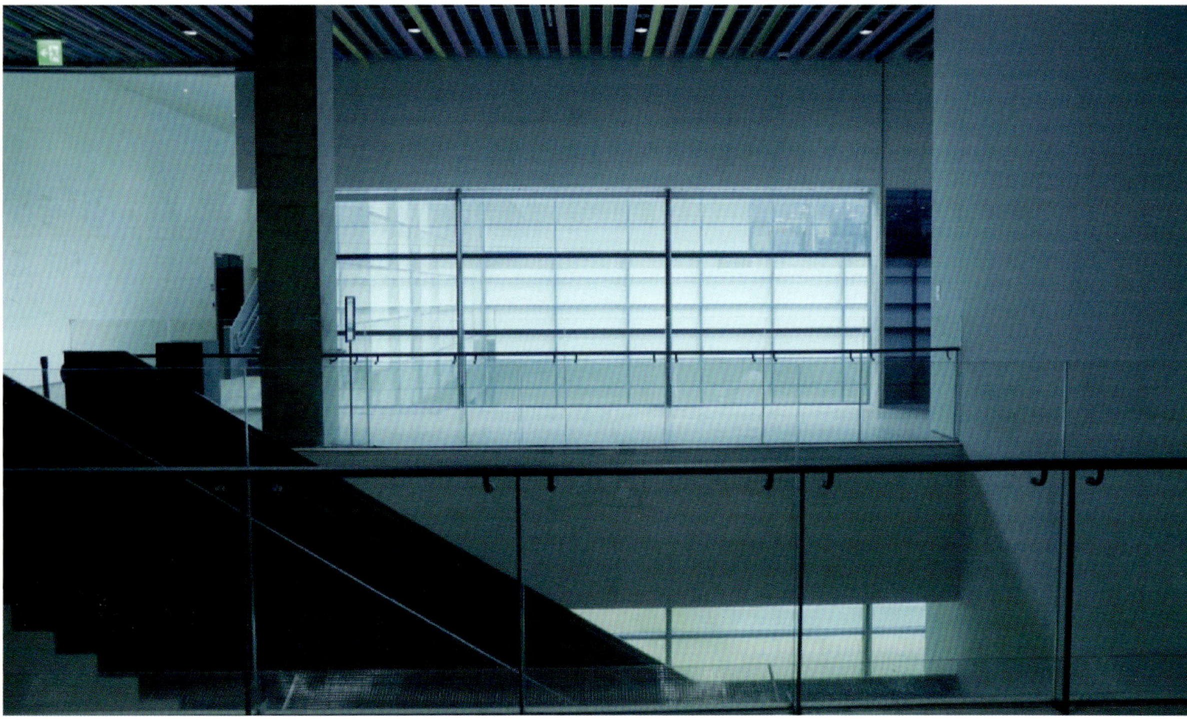

(12)

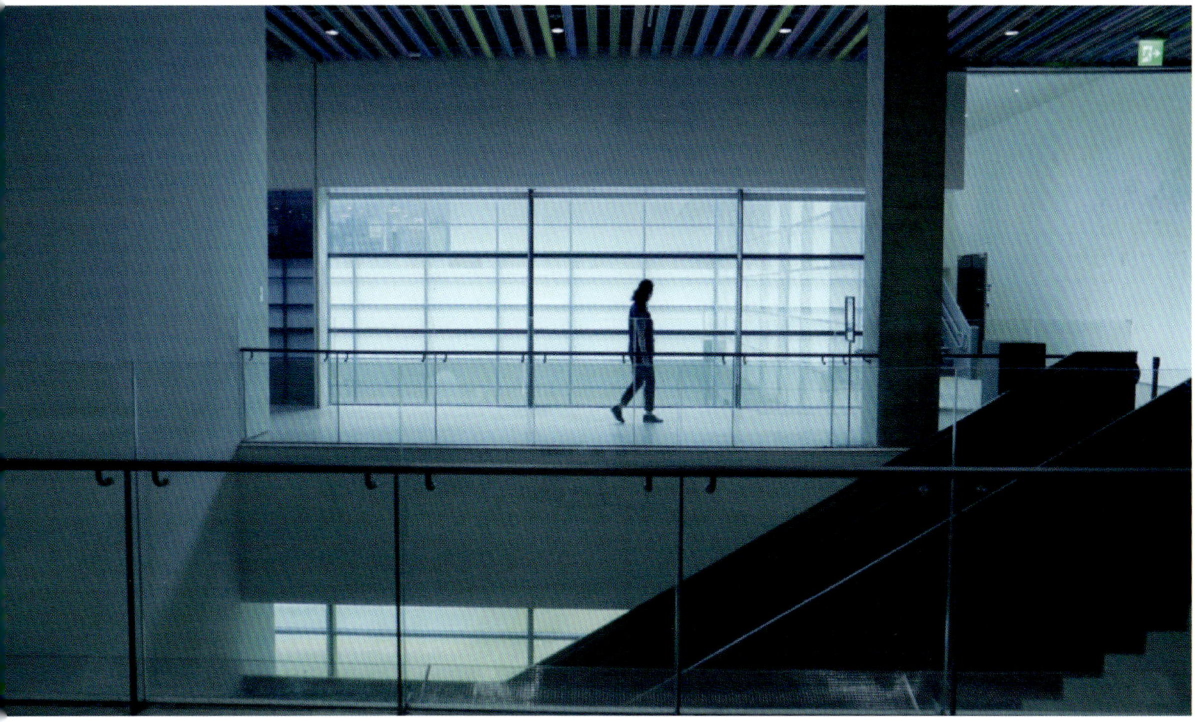

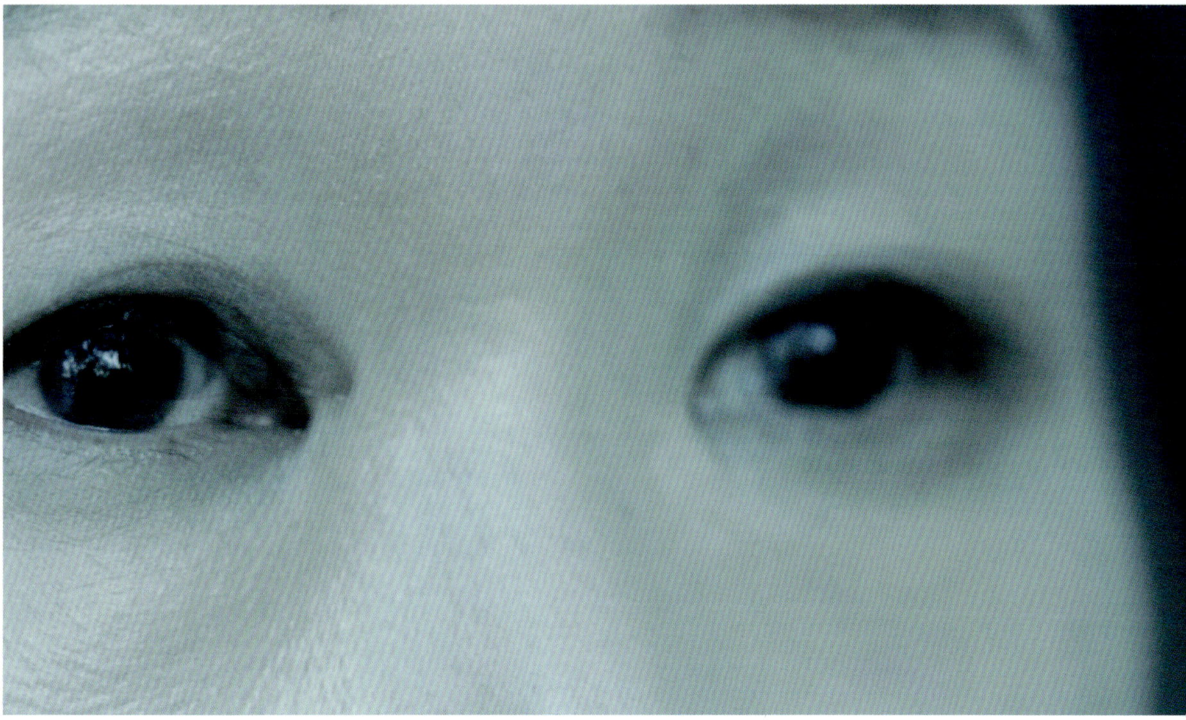

(13)

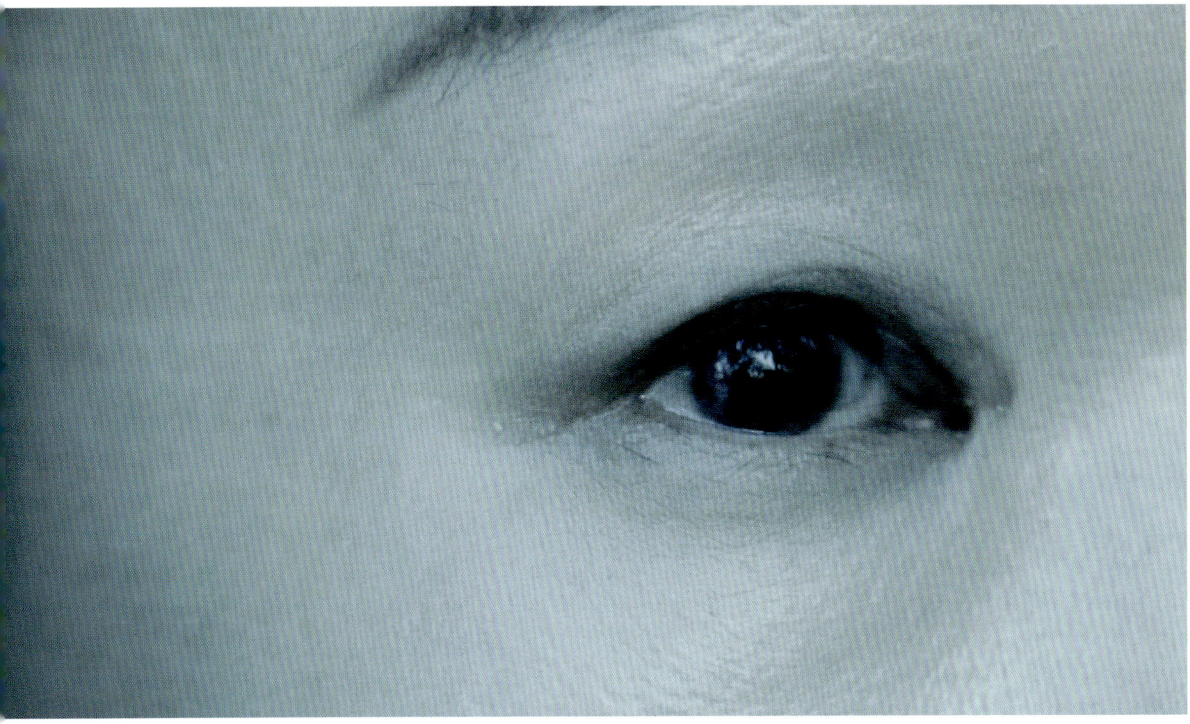

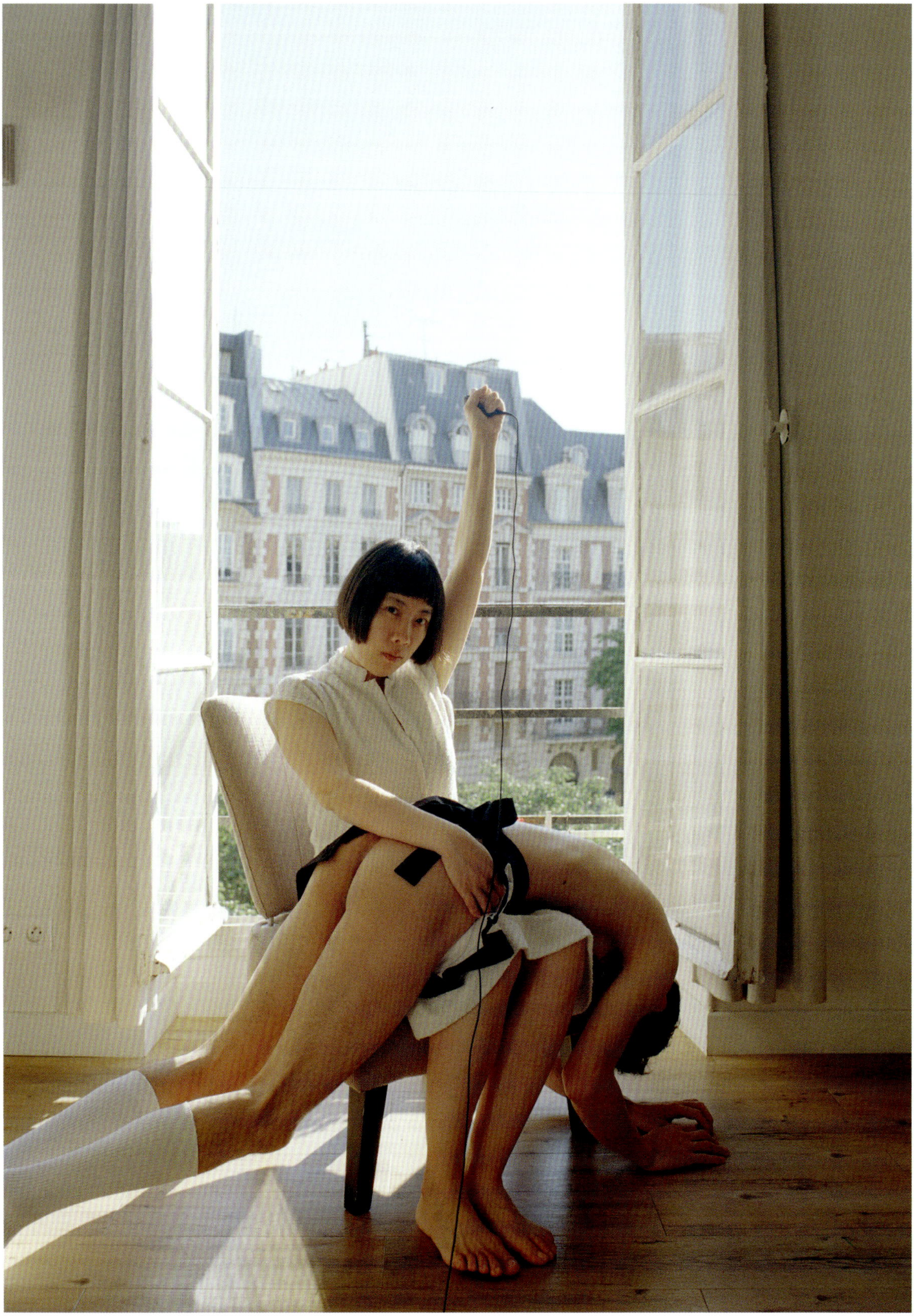

(14)

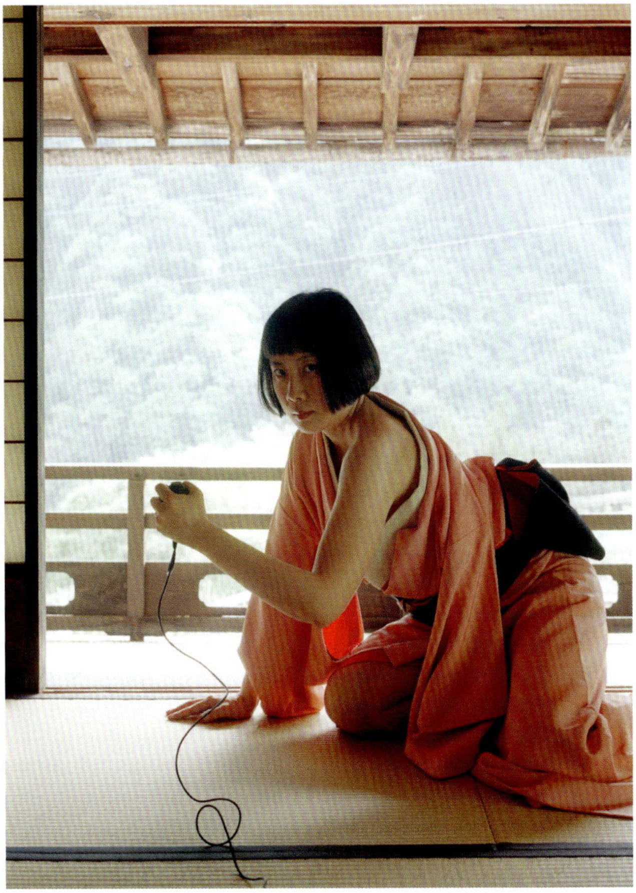

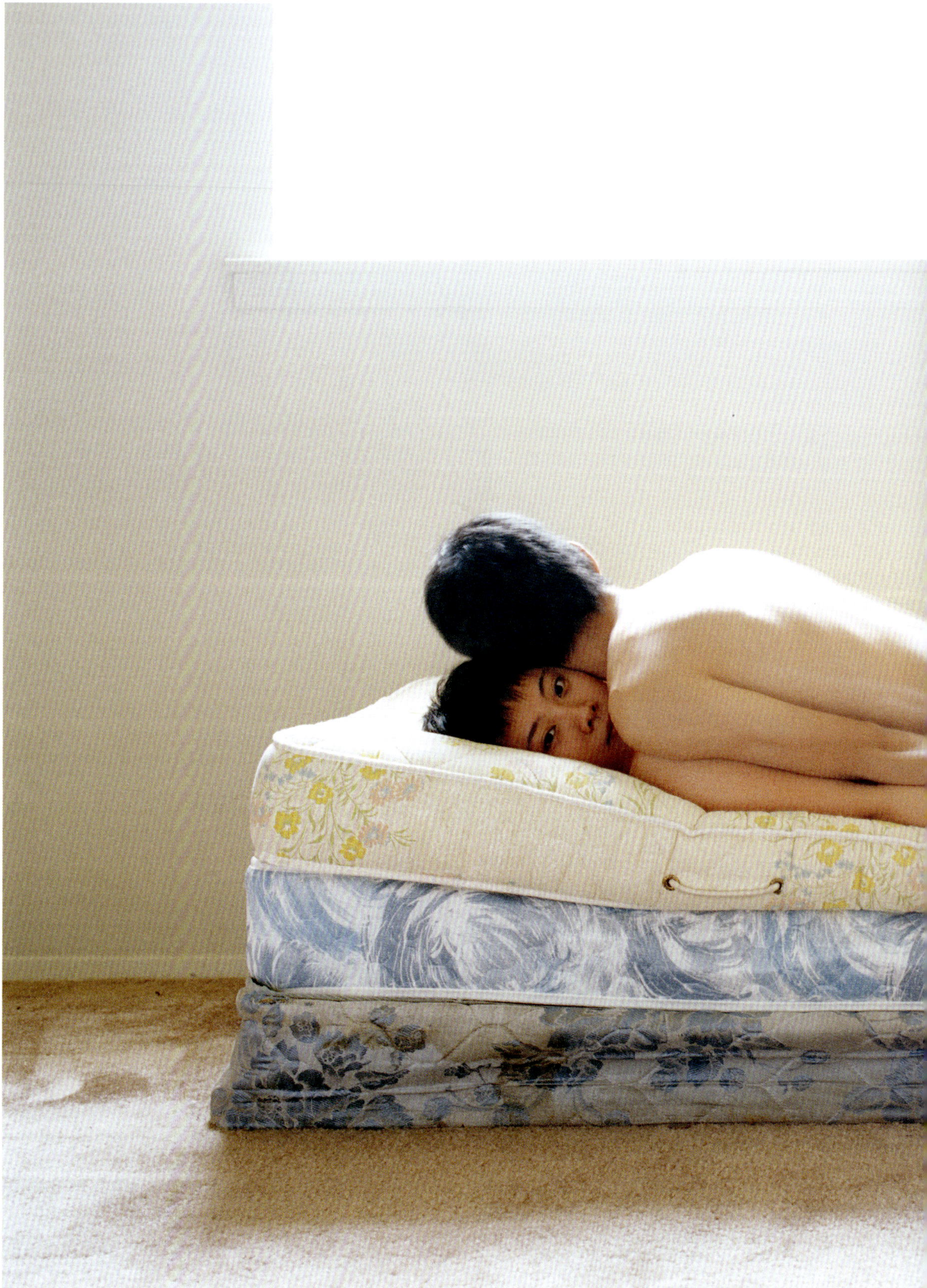

(16)

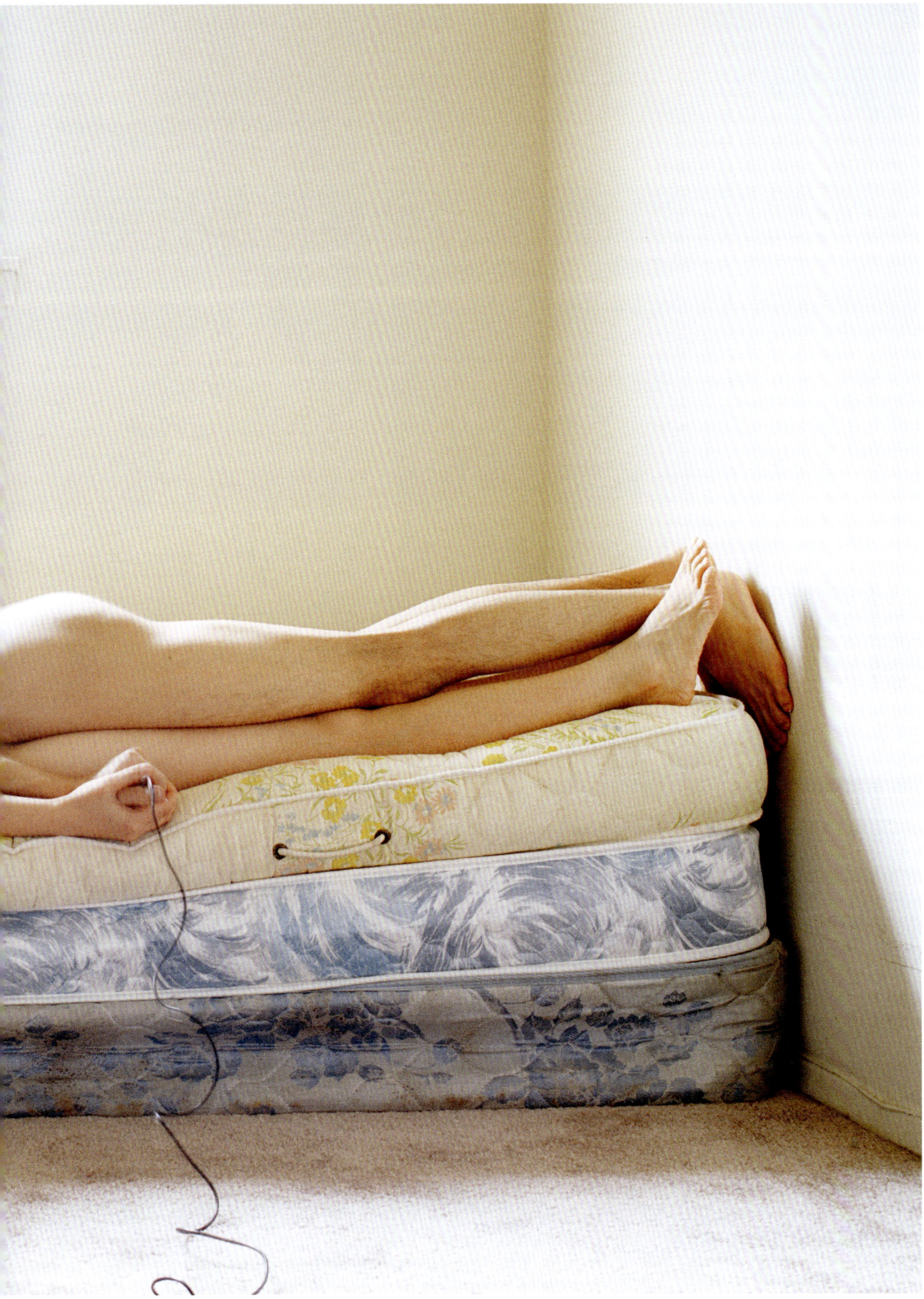

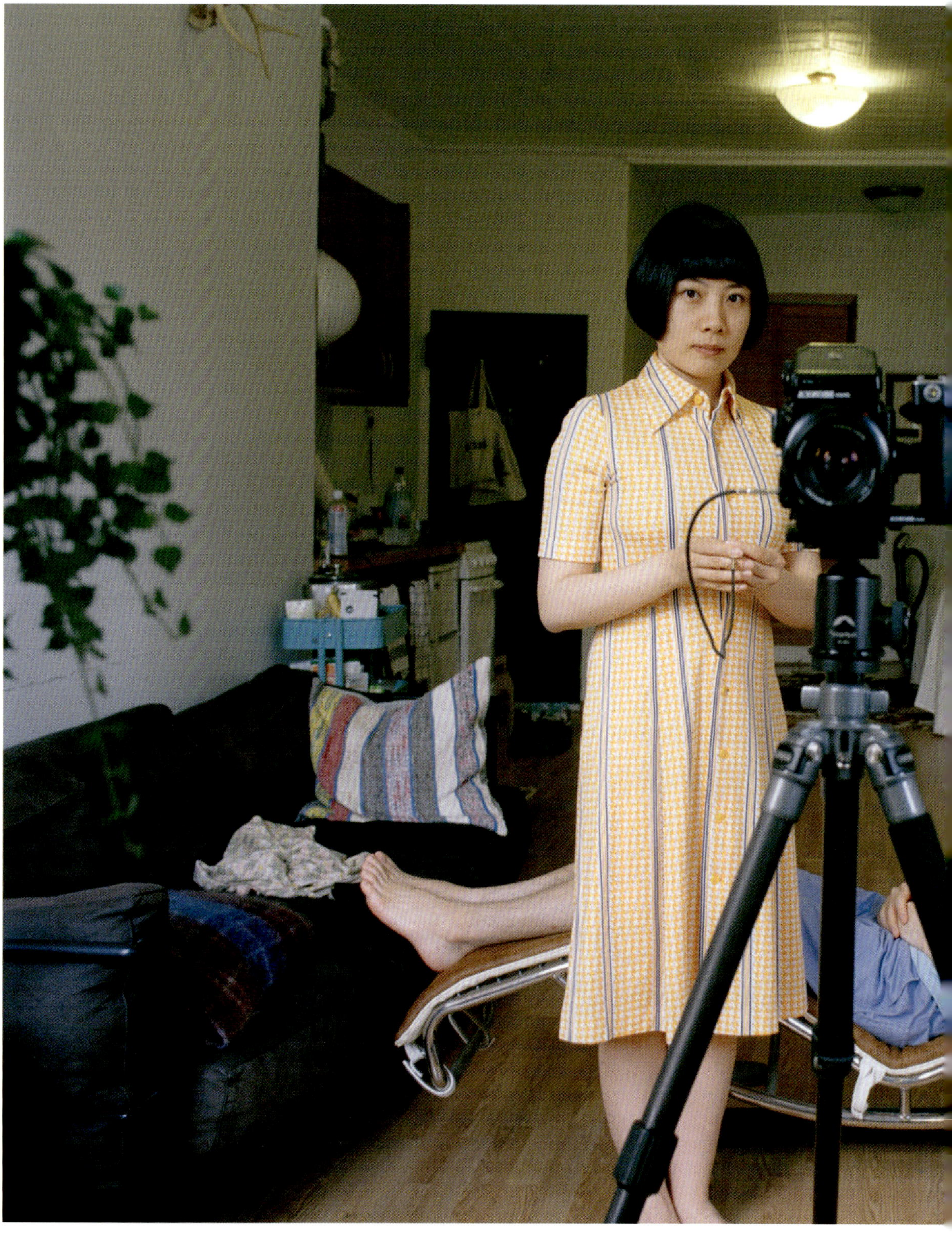

(17)

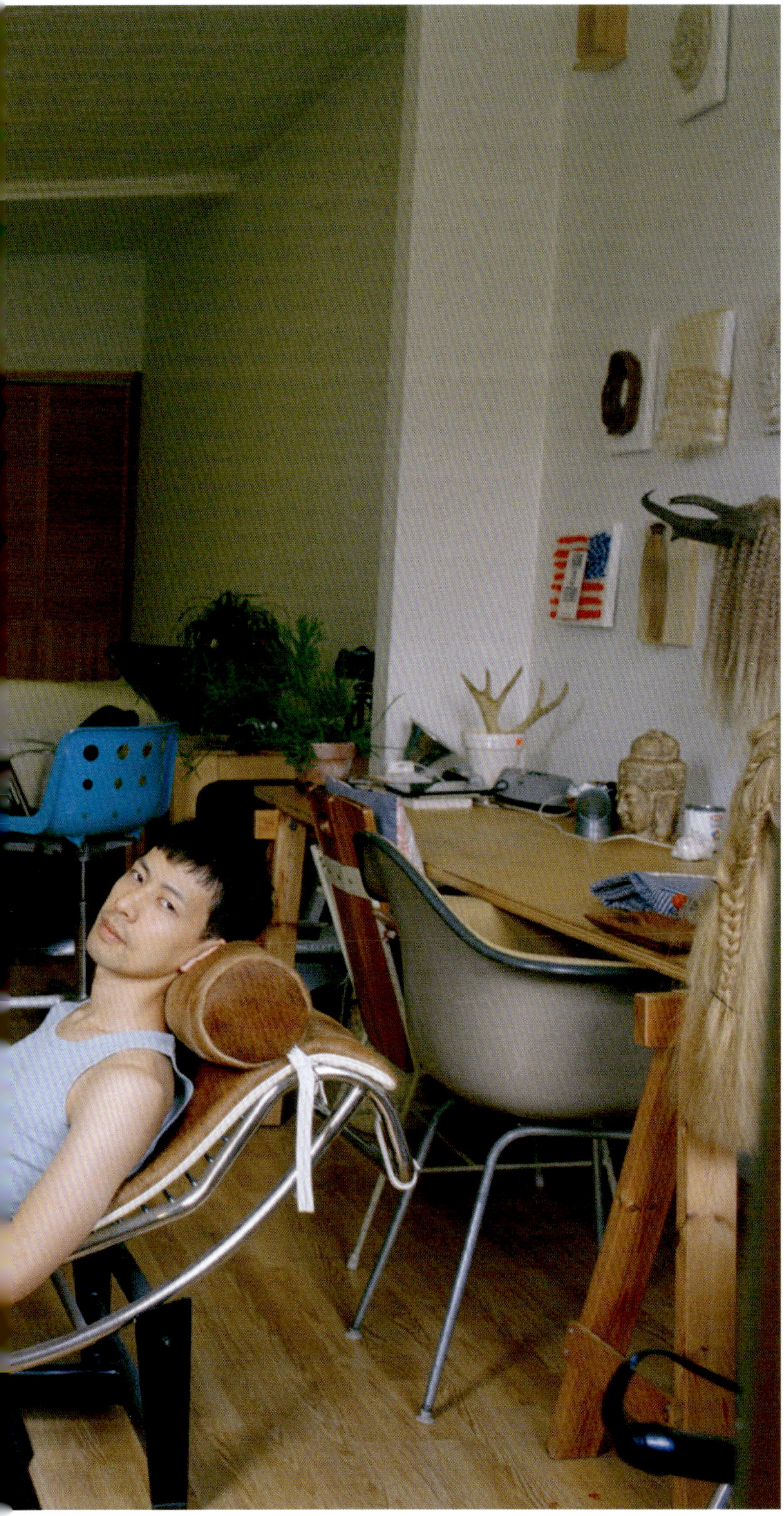

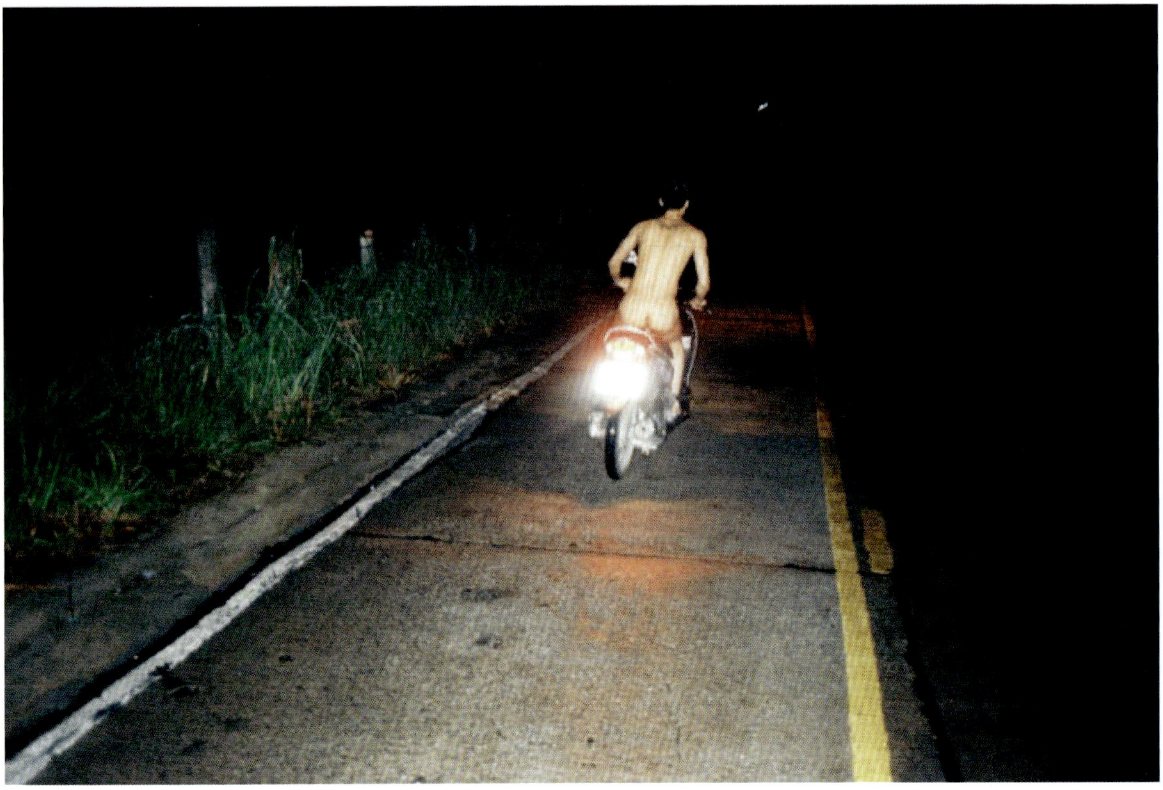

(18)

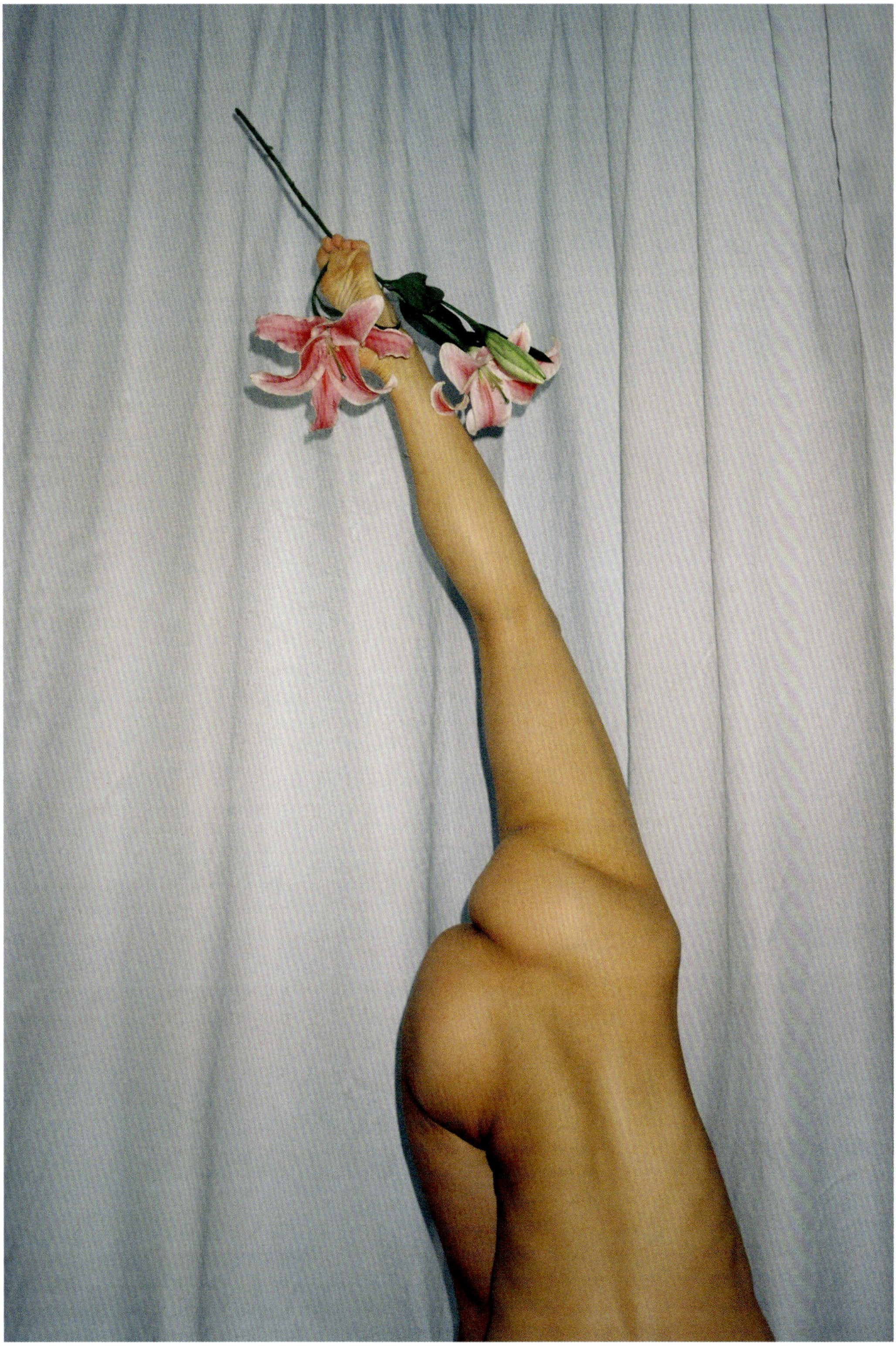

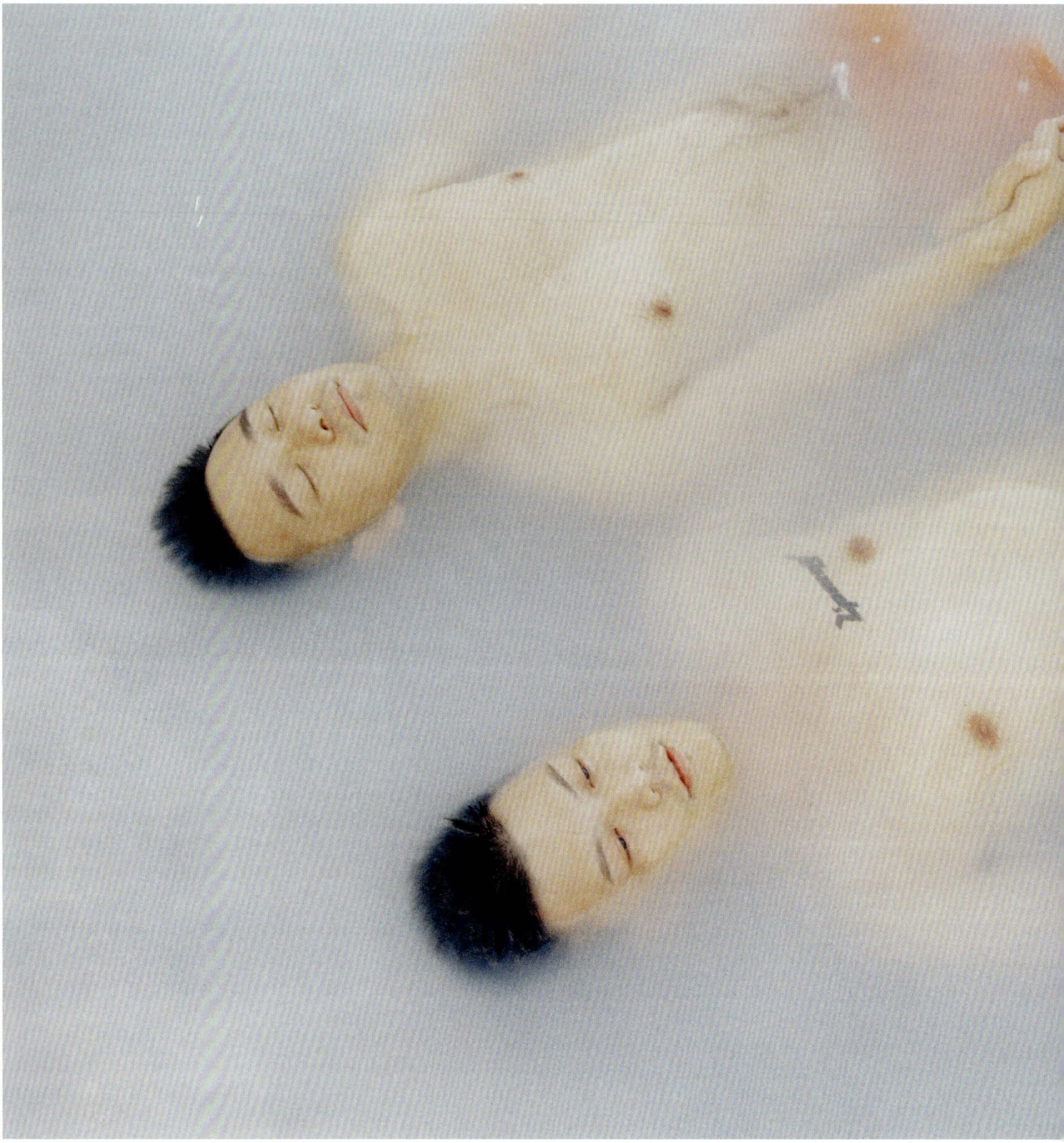

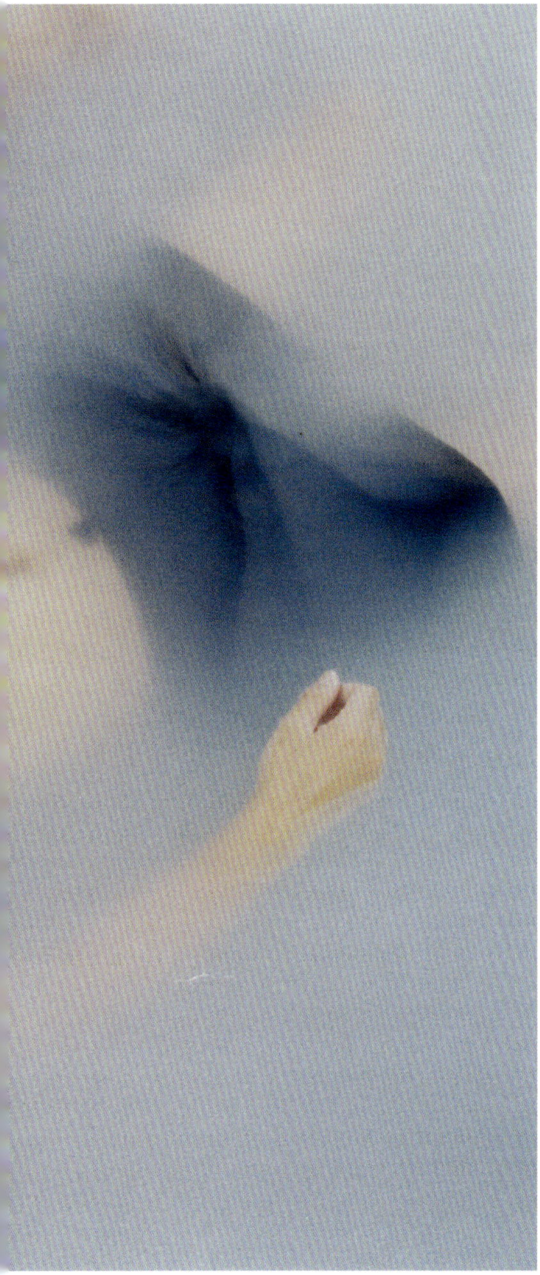

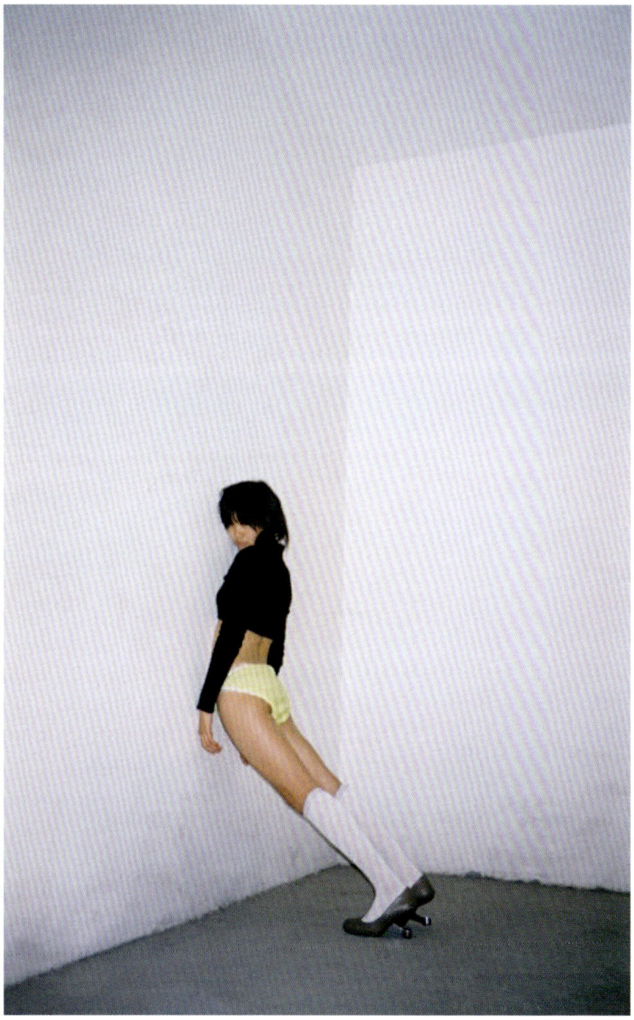

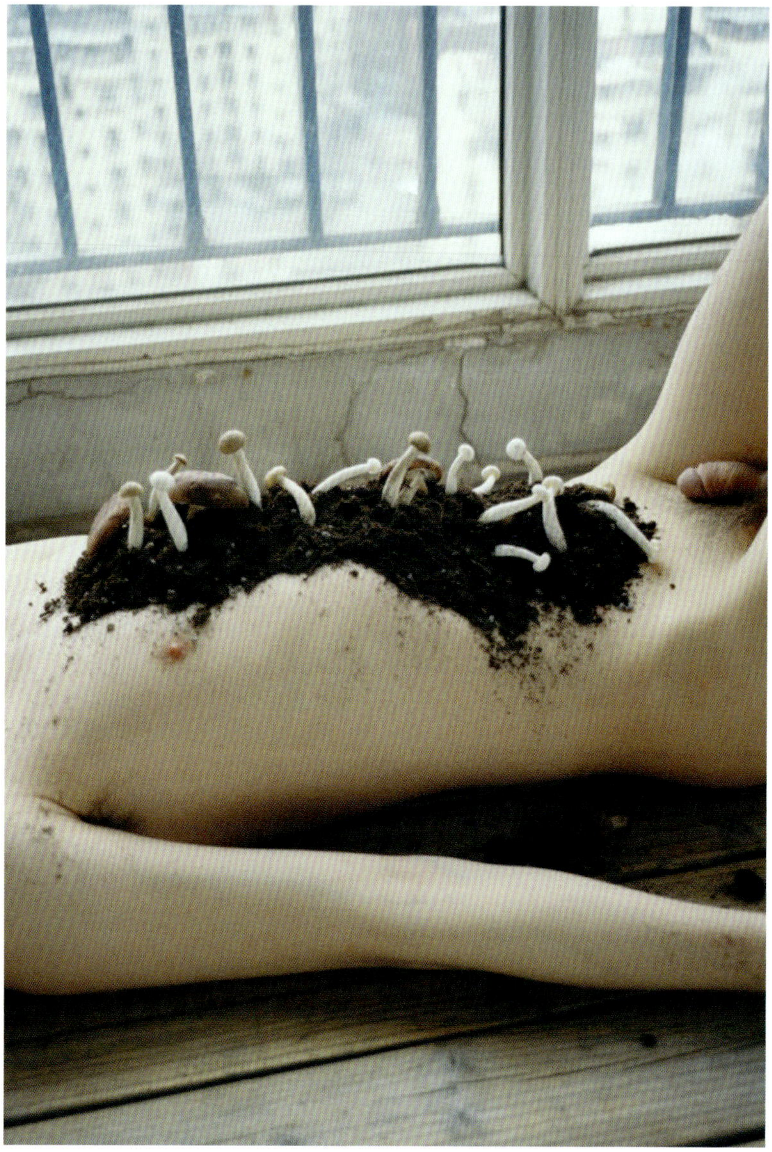

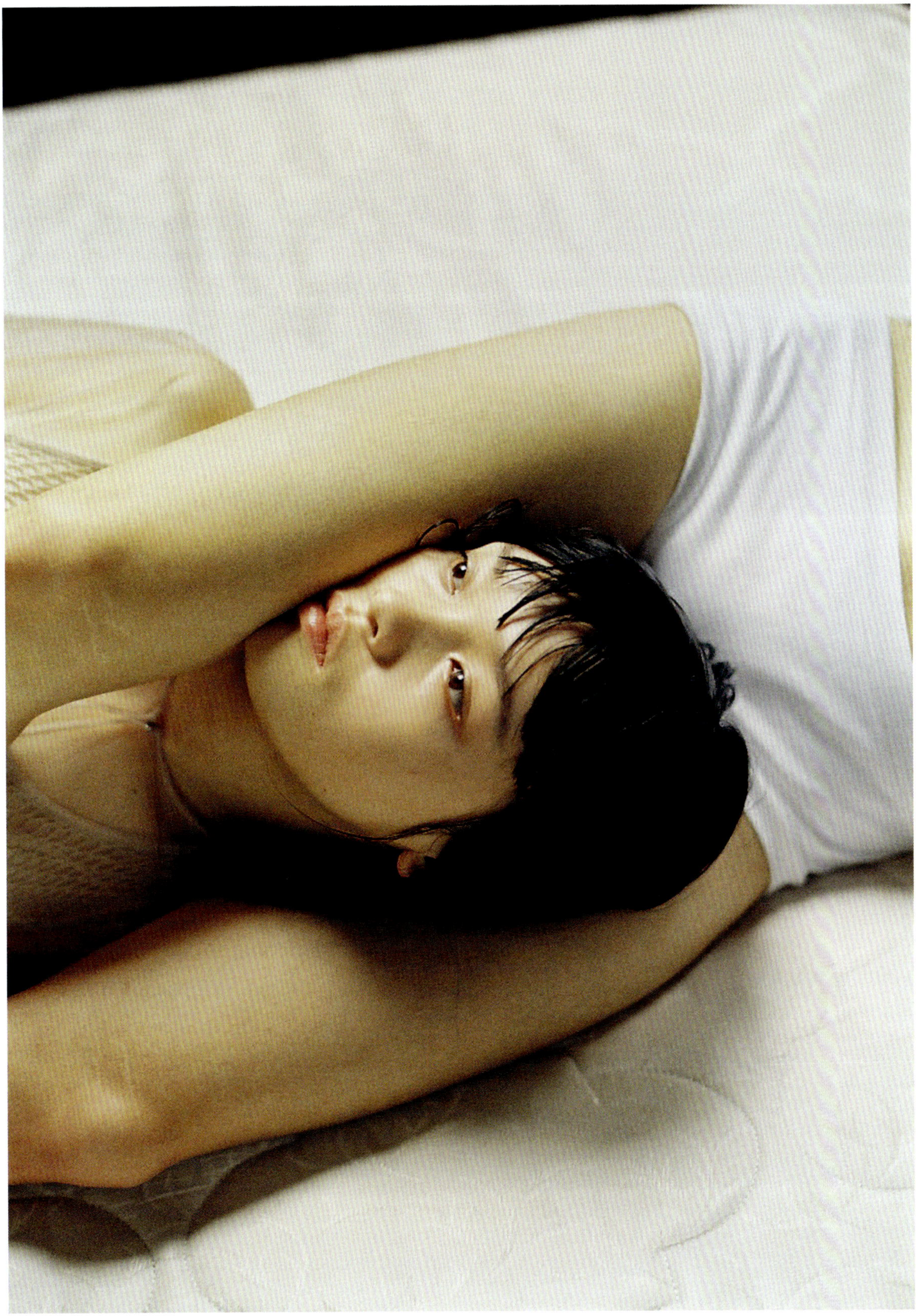

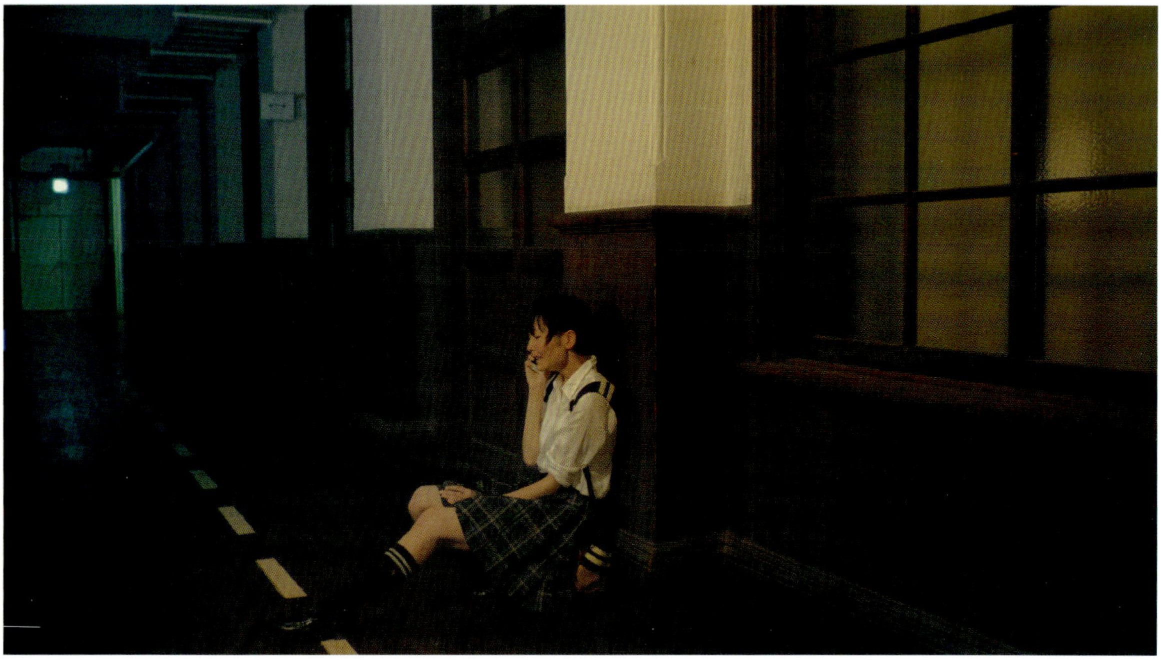

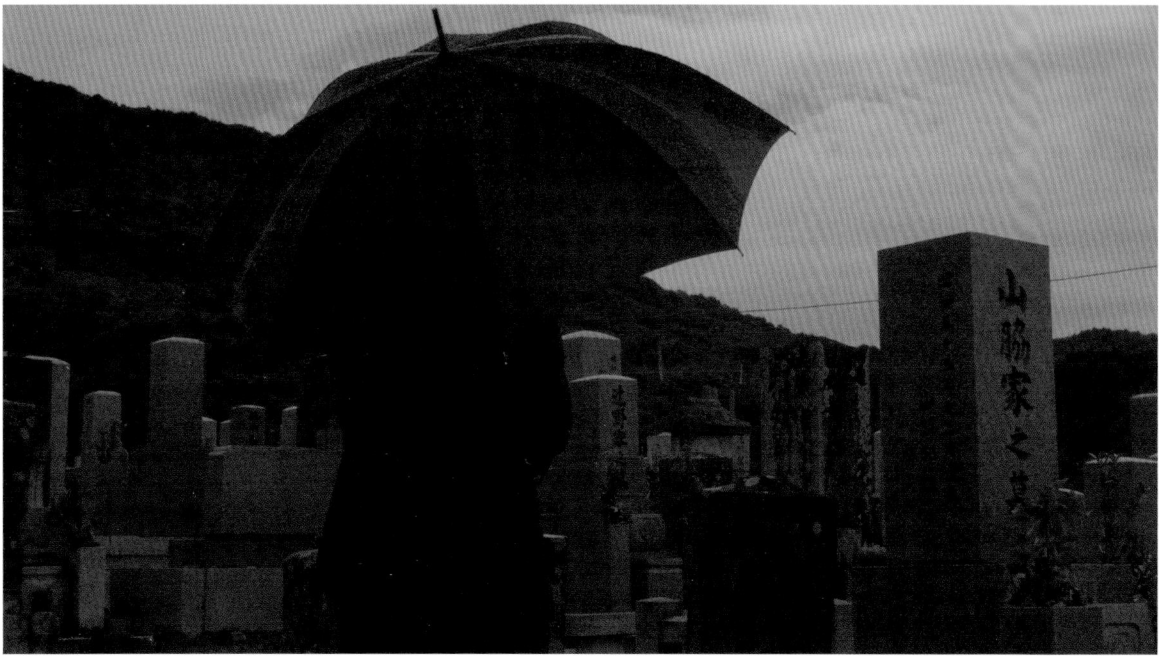

〔25〕

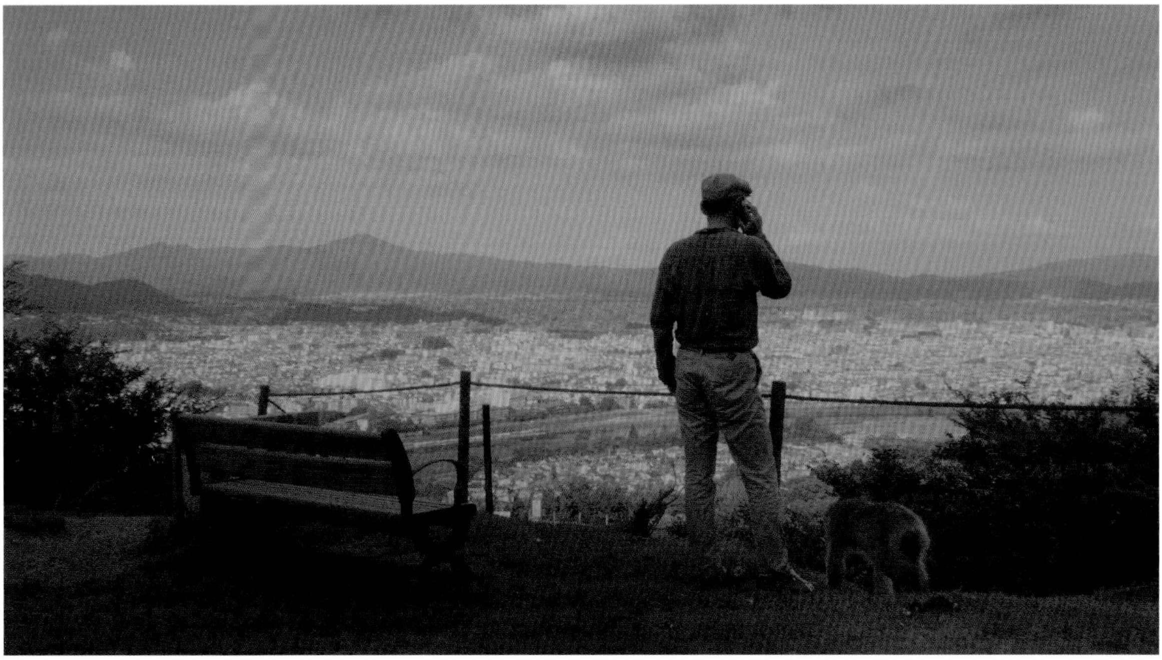

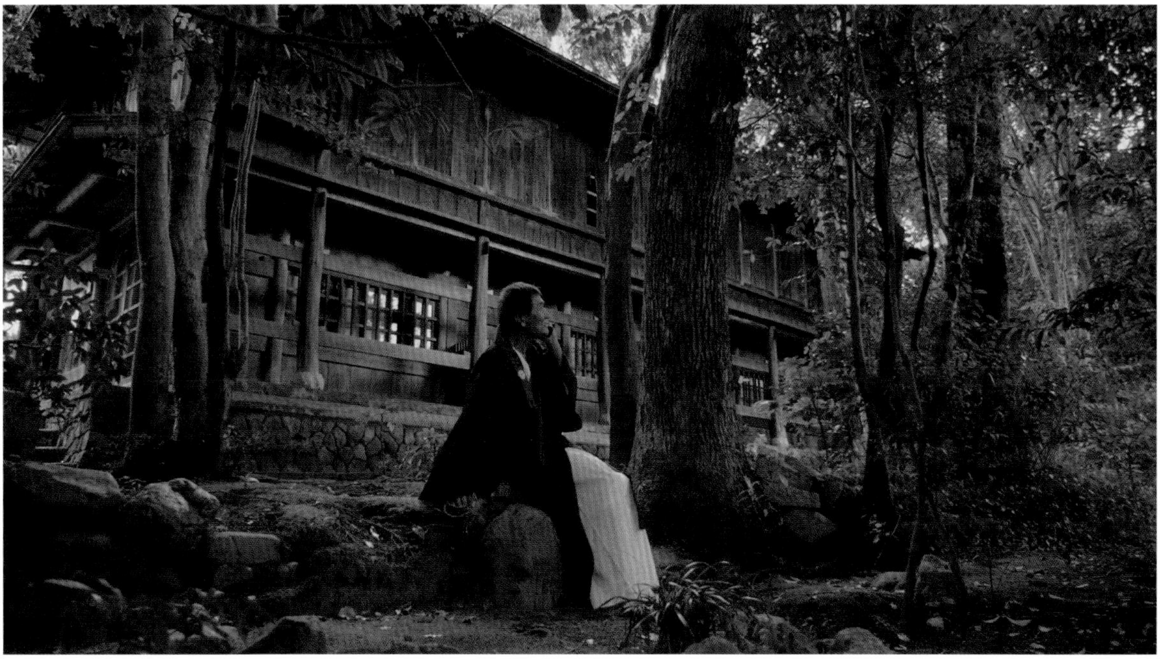

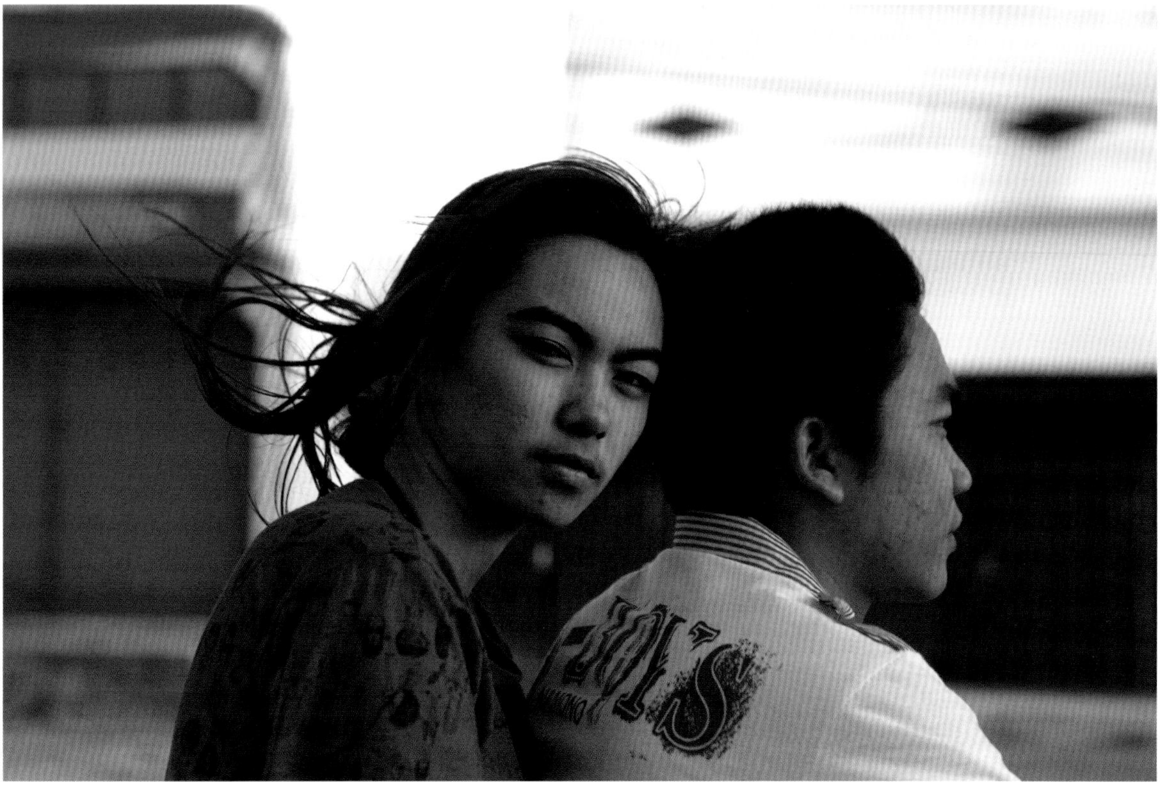

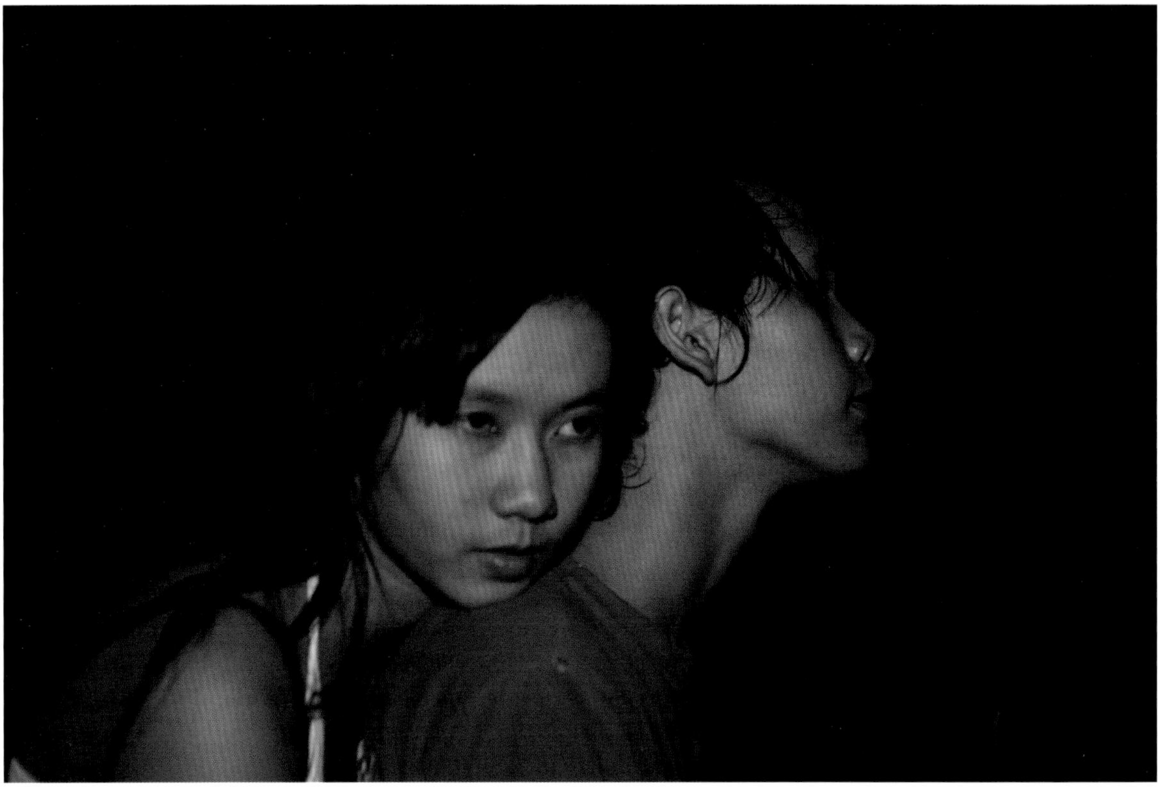

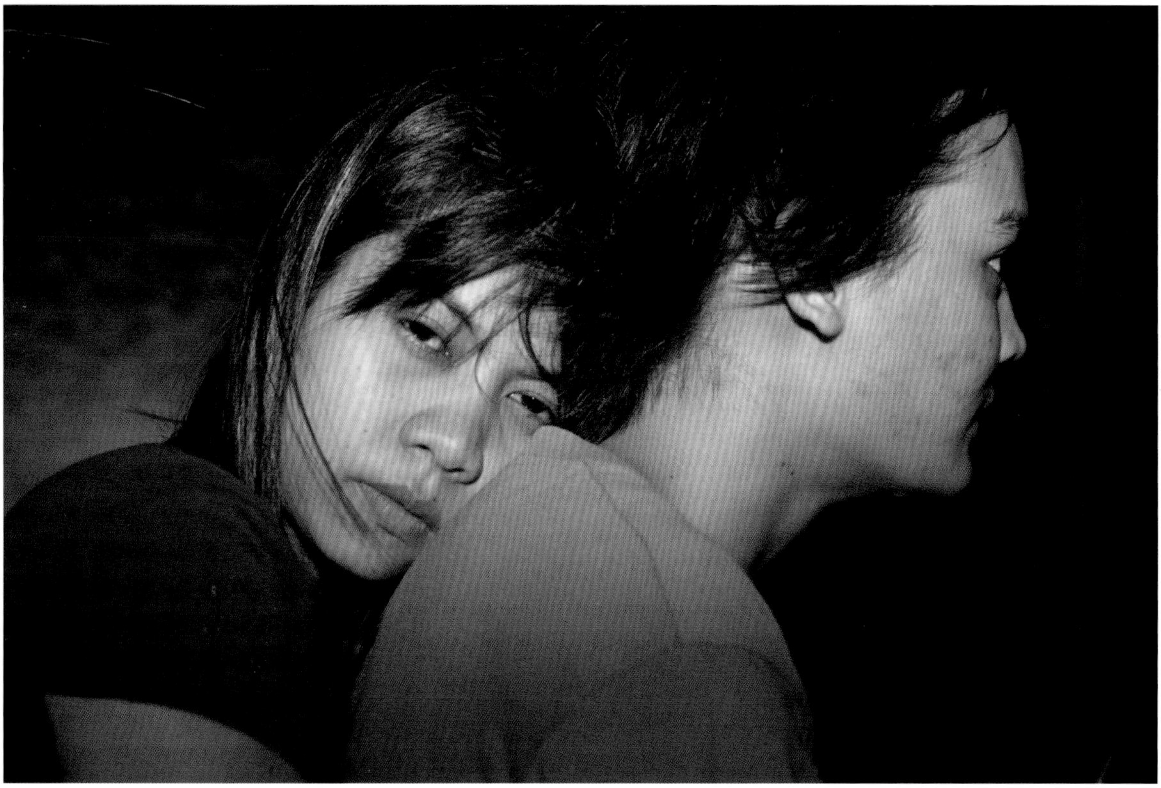

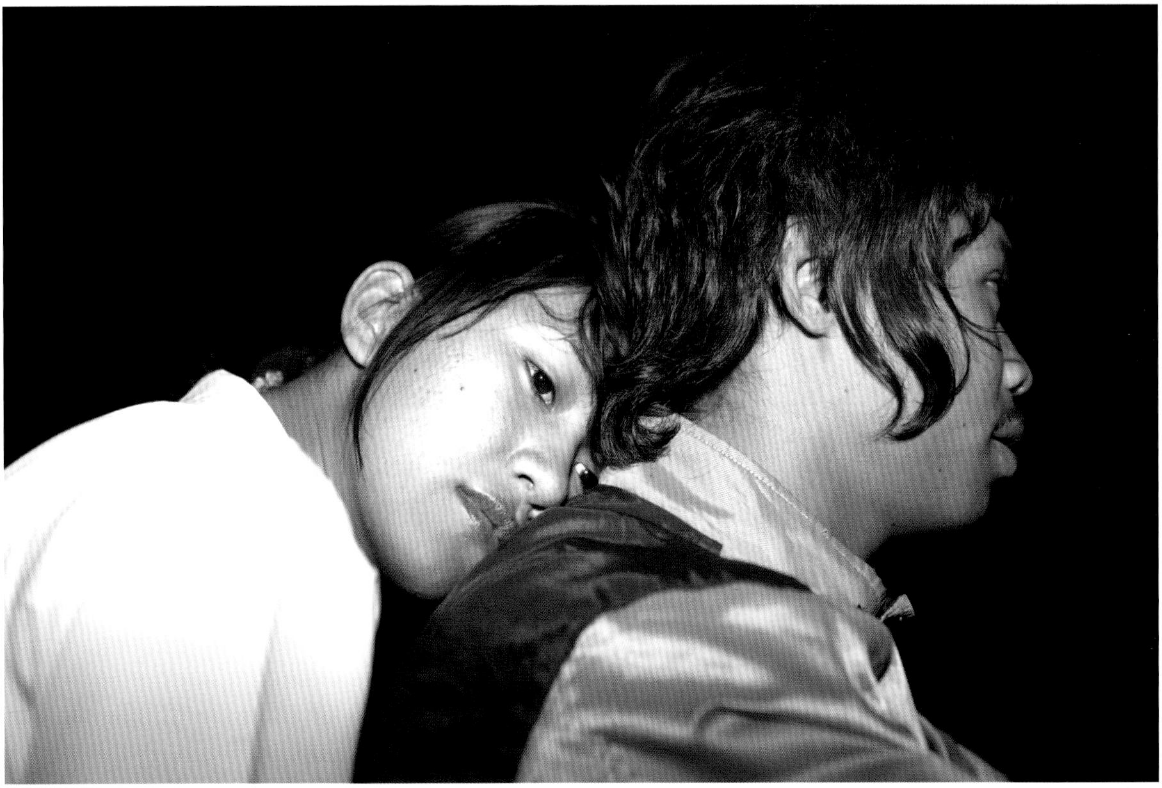

(01) Hai-Hsin Huang, *Mayday Blues #3,* 2021, oil on canvas, 53 × 45.5 cm

(02) Hai-Hsin Huang, *The Future is Hot #1,* 2021, oil on canvas, 53 × 45.5 cm

(03) Hai-Hsin Huang, *The Future is Hot #4,* 2021, oil on canvas, 53 × 45.5 cm

(04) Hai-Hsin Huang, *The Future is Hot #6,* 2021, oil on canvas, 53 × 45.5 cm

(05, 06) Daisuke Kosugi, *Recliner LC4,* 2019, bamboo, steel, plastic strips, pine, 105 × 185 × 85 cm

(07, 08) Daisuke Kosugi, *A False Weight,* 2019 (still), 4K UHD video, 5.1 ch audio, 49 minutes

(09-11) Rinko Kawauchi, *Untitled* from the series *Cui Cui,* 2005, C-type print, 30.5 × 25.4 cm

(12, 13) Sejin Kim, *Urban Hermit,* 2016 (still), 2 channel HD video, stereo sound, 6 minutes 21 seconds

(14) Pixy Liao, *After Psyche Revived by Cupid's Kiss,* 2019, digital print, 200 × 150 cm

(15) Pixy Liao, 按快门的女人 *The Woman Who Clicks The Shutter,* 2018, digital print, 200 × 150 cm

(16) Pixy Liao, *How to build a relationship with layered meanings,* 2008, digital print, 150 × 200 cm

(17) Pixy Liao, *Photographer and her muse I,* 2014, digital print, 150 × 200 cm

(18) Lin Zhipeng (aka No. 223), 假如破晓永无伏线 *Riding at Night,* 2009, archival pigment print, 33 × 50 cm

(19) Lin Zhipeng (aka No. 223), 百合之巅 *Top of Lily,* 2010, archival pigment print, 50 × 33 cm

(20) Lin Zhipeng (aka No. 223), *Couple,* 2016, archival pigment print, 134 × 200 cm

(21) Lin Zhipeng (aka No. 223), 空房间里的 *Kid In The Empty Room,* 2006, archival pigment print, 50 × 33 cm

(22) Lin Zhipeng (aka No. 223), *Mushroom Container,* 2020, archival pigment print, 50 x 33 cm

(23) Lin Zhipeng (aka No. 223), 剪刀的叙述 *Scissors' Narrative,* 2019, archival pigment print, 50 × 33 cm

(24-27) Tao Hui, *Hello, Finale!* 2017 (still), HD video installation, colour, sound, 40 minutes

(28-31) Lieko Shiga, *Untitled* from the series *Blind Date,* 2009, digital print, 60 x 90 cm

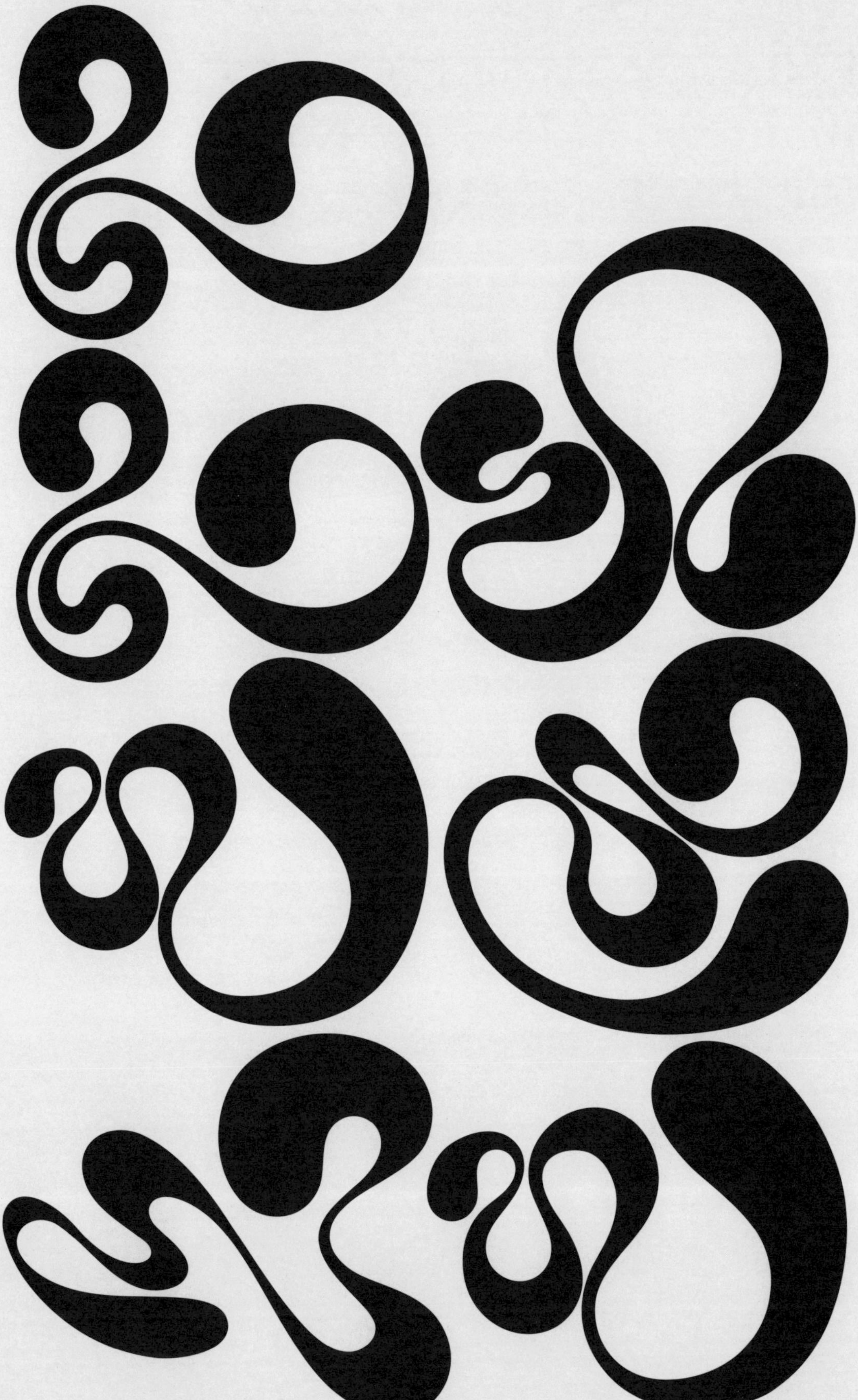

(01) For Rachel Cieśla
(02) For Hai-Hsin Huang
(03) For Daisuke Kosugi
(04) For Rinko Kawauchi
(05) For Sejin Kim
(06) For Pixy Liao
(07) For Lin Zhipeng (aka No.223)
(08) For Tao Hui

Biljana Ciric

Biljana Ciric

Biljana Ciric is an interdependent curator based in Belgrade. Her recent exhibitions include Vladimir Nikolić: Walking with Water, Pavilion of the Republic of Serbia, 59th Venice Biennale, 2022; Repetition as a Gesture Towards Deep Listening, Trans-Southeast Asia Triennial, Guangzhou, 2021; Modes of Encounter: An Inquiry, Guangzhou Times Museum, 2019; Proposals to Surrender, McAM, Shanghai, 2016; Everything You Need To Know About The FY Art Foundation: An Exhibition, FY Art Foundation space, Shen Zhen, 2017. She was co-curator of the 3rd Ural Industrial Biennial for Contemporary Art, Yekaterinburg in 2015.

(01) Rachel Cieśla

Rachel Cieśla is the Lead Creative for the Simon Lee Foundation Institute of Contemporary Asian Art at The Art Gallery of Western Australia, Boorloo/Perth.

Dear Rachel

Three years into the pandemic, while looking at the works you are planning to exhibit, I could empathise with the loneliness and loss that many of the works reflect upon. In some moments, that recognition felt very physical somewhere deep inside my stomach.

In her book *Woman, Native, Other*, Trinh T. Minh-ha writes that throughout Asia many cultures understand three centers in the human being: the intellectual (*path*), connected to reason; the emotional (*oth*), connected to the heart; and the vital (*kath*). Located below the navel, the kath center, Minh-ha says, 'radiates life'. It directs vital movement and allows one to relate to the world with instinctual immediacy.[1] I try to write from this centre below the navel – that very place that does not separate body from mind nor heart and is infused by consciousness. Minh-ha proposes thinking of consciousness not as an accumulation of knowledge and experience but as ongoing unsettling processes. I am trying to inscribe unsettling processes into the practice of letter writing. [2]

Writing letters negotiates an expectation of intimacy.[3] Letters also propose certain relational aspects – aspects of self-healing and care towards one another [4] that extend to a community that might read this letter but never make it to the site to see the exhibition. By community, here, I mean all of us who, in the last three years, have investigated the question of where we are heading and what our future will unfold. I am also referring to communities that have been living on this planet for thousands of years, and who are trying to answer the question of how to be a better ancestor. Writing letters is an attempt to diminish the distance and authority of writing. I always felt uncomfortable writing about artists and their works from a distance. My response always went in the opposite direction – towards a certain proximity and relation. When I write about someone's work, I rarely find satisfaction in critical writing and its format of authority that we usually take for granted.

Letters remind us that, besides a dominant history that goes back to the Republic of Letters in the seventeenth and eighteenth centuries (usually related to 'men of letters'), important historical studies have uncovered a network of early women of letters who were engaged in intellectual debate both among themselves and with the men.[5] These exchanges were central to feminist networks and ideas, and this history has slowly been re-valued as a model for feminist futures. Letter writing is part of feminist politics. For me, it is also a pathway towards new art histories, providing a means to progress in times when we continue to be separated and struggle to understand each other's realities.

I have spent some time talking with each artist in the exhibition through Zoom. I wanted to hear them speak. To hear their voices and

1. Trinh T. Minh-ha *Woman Native, Other, Writing Postcoloniality and Feminism* (Bloomington: Indiana University press, 1989), 40.

2. Minh-ha, *Woman, Native, Other*, 40.

3. Margaretta Jolly, *In Love and Struggle: Letters of Contemporary Feminism* (New York: Columbia University press, 2010), 1.

4. Jolly, *In Love*, 111

5. Alex Martinis Roe, *To Become Two: Propositions for Feminist Collective Practice* (Berlin: Archive Books, 2018), 168.

their silence. To understand their realities and their struggle through the Zoom square. To glimpse the private space behind them. To get closer.

'During pandemic lockdowns everyone lived lives like ours,' Pixy Liao said during our conversation.[6] What does this sentence say about cultural practitioners? What kinds of lives have we been living? For some, staying home during the pandemic could be considered a privilege, revealing a clear class division between those who can work from home and those who can't. Marco Baravalle has defined us cultural workers as a nomadic, superficially sympathetic, and often ruthless international community.[7] Most of us work from our homes unless we're travelling for an exhibition or residency in which we temporarily inhabit another place and context. He invites us to practice radical permanence rather than nomadism. For him, radical permanence doesn't mean an absence of mobility, rather it invites us to think and practice mobility from an ecological point of view.[8]

6. Pixy Liao in conversation with the author, May 23, 2022.

7. Marco Baravalle, 'On the Biennale's ruins? Inhabiting the void, covering the distance,' trans. Gabriella Riccio, Institute of Radical Imagination, May 2, 2020

8. Baravalle, 'On the Biennale's ruins?', 12.

Think of exhibition-making. Is it possible for an exhibition to be a sustainable endeavor? The way we have been accustomed to making exhibitions has been highly unsustainable. What is the future of these practices, and how can we establish an ethical relationship with place without becoming provincial or feeling we are missing out on connections that form and inform our thinking beyond one place? I believe that we are deeply colonised in our way of thinking and doing, and this is something that will take generations to unlearn. It is unlearning in order to be a different kind of human, but also a different kind of curator or artist.

Decolonisation is a slow process, but we need to acknowledge the importance of every step we collectively take in that direction – no matter how small and unimpressive it might be. We need to move away from the exhibition ritual as core to our practice and move towards different kinds of encounters. We need different vocabularies to talk about what we do and to be brave about naming. We also need to learn that failure is part of the decolonising process. We need to feel comfortable with falling, with standing up and continuing. Realising this made me appreciate Charlie Chaplin much more – understanding his seemingly clumsy moves as an opposition to mechanical actions and 'normal' ways of inhabiting space.

Curators needs to take such falls. We need to learn with Chaplin about not being afraid of being laughed at, of being vulnerable. Can we make an exhibition in which we fall badly, break a leg and break an exhibition?

I struggle to imagine it.
It would be such an important interruption of our ritual.
Maybe we start with a modest fall.
A fall is a fall. [9]

9. Unpublished notes by Biljana Ciric on curatorial methodologies, 2020.

Biljana Ciric

(02) Hai-Hsin Huang

Hai-Hsin Huang (born 1984, Taipei, Taiwan; lives Taipei) works primarily with painting, drawing, and publications. Capturing the awkward and unglamorous moments of daily life through a sardonic lens, Huang creates ambiguous narratives that fall somewhere between humour and horror. Her work stems from what she described as 'frustrating life experiences', depicting the tension between reality with the idealised versions of life that we construct from the everyday.

After graduating from the National Taipei University of Education in 2007, Huang relocated to New York, where she obtained her MFA from the School of Visual Arts in 2009. Huang has exhibited at the Museum of Fine Arts, Leipzig (2017); Juming Museum, Taipei (2019); Mori Art Museum, Tokyo (2018); Seoul Museum of Art (2018); National Taiwan Museum of Fine Arts, Taichung (2016); and Taipei Fine Arts Museum (2013).

For Hai-Hsin Huang

Hai-Hsin Huang was in Taipei when we spoke. It was afternoon for her and the weather in Taipei was humid with no sunshine for days. She noted that such weather is very uninspiring. This is also how she described her inner weather. Behind her I could see the beginnings of a new work.

Dear Huang Hai Hsin,

Windows seem important. You told me that whenever you don't know what to paint you look through the window. From the window your gaze enters other people's lives. You are the observer, but also the filter, as you said. You told me you understand the role of an artist as a filter that conveys the emotion we all have but are not allowed to point out.

You are a distant observer not an intruder. Windows were an important way out during lockdown – resting your eyes, looking at the buildings and the lives that unfold close to yours.

You continued to work during lockdown – at ease in the knowledge that you did not have to worry that you were missing out. You diligently created one drawing per day, imagining what other people, locked in apartments, were doing. You didn't finish the notebook with the planned 365 drawings. You stopped at 124. It remained incomplete for many reasons, I imagine, perhaps the main one being that our knowledge and experience is fragmented and patchy like our understanding of others.[10] Could it also be your own struggle to imagine otherwise?[11] I forgot to ask you. For me there is a certain beauty when a painter doesn't finish a work.

The future for all of us was, and still is, hard to imagine. When the pandemic started, your disappointment about uncovering the other side of humanity was present in your apocalyptic paintings of humans in artificial environments – in deserts, with fires raging while life continues on as usual. These images almost resample our reality today. I am planning summer holidays while the Ukraine war is still happening. Sometimes I think I'm crazy.

You leave space for hope through a kid flying a kite, or a man playing the piano. Your work follows your (or our) actions. You turned to self-care as a mechanism to cope with lockdown depression. You turn to self-care in order to be close to us – the middle class that you may belong to, but always hold a mirror up to. You told me a few times

10. Donna Haraway, 'Situated Knowledges: The Science Question in Feminism and the Privilege of Partial Perspective,' *Feminist Studies* 14, no. 3 (1988), 584.

11. See Haraway, 'Situated Knowledges'.

that you are no different from others. You are us. Museum settings are replaced in your recent paintings by scenes of gymnastics and hiking. You are actively participating in both. You go to gymnastics classes and buy expensive hiking gear.

In your works reciprocity and attentiveness to detail reveal a strong discomfort, reminding us of the failure of our collective capacity to overcome the commercialisation of our anxieties.

In your painting you insist that we see what we usually don't want to see and I thank you for that.

Biljana Ciric

(03) Daisuke Kosugi

Daisuke Kosugi (born 1984, Tokyo, Japan; lives Farsund, Norway) works with film, performance, text, sound, and sculpture to express dislocated subjectivities within a normalised social milieu. Through layers of fiction and non-fiction, Kosugi constructs seductive scenarios that entail an underlying conflict between personal freedom and systems. Questioning the role of empathy in contemporary society, Kosugi often works closely with his family members and other individuals to explore their inner lives, guiding audiences through intimate experiences where conflict is rendered bodily and emotionally.

Kosugi graduated with a Bachelor of Fine Art at the Academy of Fine Art, Oslo National Academy of the Arts, in 2014. Kosugi has had solo exhibitions at the Jeu de Paume, Paris (2019); CAPC musée d'art contemporain de Bordeaux (2019); Museo Amparo, Puebla (2019); and Fotogalleriet, Oslo (2019). His work has also been exhibited at Whitechapel Gallery, London (2020); Bonniers Konsthall, Stockholm (2020); Centre Pompidou, Paris (2019); CPH:DOX, Copenhagen (2017); and the 11th Gwangju Biennale (2016).

For Daisuke Kosugi

Daisuke was in a small town in the north of Norway where he had recently relocated to start life with a new partner. His outside weather was winter. He was wearing a thick jacket during our conversation. Indoors must have been cold as well. He explained that often in the north it happens that one day in summer, all of a sudden it feels like winter. His inner weather was chaotic, as he described it – full of animals and children.

Dear Daisuke,

I imagine that the world of children is also full of sounds. Sounds that somehow create a space to imagine feral creatures inviting other critters to join in or not. It is in that very space of the feral where stories can be told differently. Donna Haraway reminds us that those stories could be fables containing wild facts. She calls them fabulous narration. Is it possible that is what you are living now? What Haraway describes are not narratives and situations that are domesticated by literary theory, but fabulations of worlding, full of different critters, encounters and situations.[12]

12. Donna Haraway, *Story Telling for Earthly Survival*, directed by Fabrizio Terranova, 2016. 1:21.

Sound is very different to language. We are so accustomed to articulating things through language and to speaking up. You told me about the influence that the book *The Body in Pain* by Elaine Scarry has had on you. After talking together about our own lack of linguistic ability to describe body pain, I thought about the role of silence in relation to the articulation of pain.

In her beautiful book *The Shape of Sound* Fiona Murphy reminds us that deaf people feel and see sound and that their entire body becomes a receptor. Imagining the body as a receptor is like visualising it as a vessel. Ursula K. Le Guin talks about our body as a carrier bag that collects plants, seeds, nuts, berries and other fruit needed for our survival.

What kind of vessel does our body become when we start enduring pain and losing the connection between mind and body? What happens to all those beautiful things that you have collected in the vessel? The nuts and fruit and bark? All those things that you are supposed to share with others – where do they end up going? Recently I listened to Brian Eno's interesting observations on airport music. Due to his fear of flying, he created a piece of ambient music for airports which tried to deconstruct the importance of our individual existence in the world.

Maybe our vessels are not important as individual entities. Perhaps what is important is what gets transmitted from vessel to vessel in the future and the past – how much of your vessel you share with others and how. Maybe the question is: *How to be a good ancestor?*

You are committed to the deep listening and intimacy that this process of transmission creates. Your methodology of working with family members through art projects over several years, reveals a willingness to stay vulnerable to the process that you propose to them and that can only arise from working with someone very close to you. Working with family members requires you to nurture not only a working relationship during the filming process, but also kinship and emotional connectedness. And that space that you nurture has become essential to your work. You are also aware that you need to continue to nurture the relationship itself after filming is complete.

You describe the work with your father as a process of grief – the decay of the body. I also see that your work has initiated and enabled a space to access an understanding of the relationship between son and father. I imagine your father never or rarely went to museums and has probably never seen your work in an exhibition. You have created a space where the process of transferring fruit and nuts into each other's vessels can happen for both of you.

I lost my grandmother in 2020. She was my guardian and someone I always returned to. I am learning to start the day by looking deep into my eyes and seeing her in myself. Have you tried to find your father in your eyes?

Biljana Ciric

〔04〕 Rinko Kawauchi

Rinko Kawauchi (born 1972, Shiga, Japan; lives Tokyo, Japan) is a photographer known for her poetic depictions of everyday life. Fascinated with the pictorial potential of the most mundane things, her photographs recreate the familiar as strange and new. Kawauchi works in series, which – in the form of open narratives – combine poetry and emotion with representations of mortality and occasional melancholy.

Kawauchi graduated from Seian University of Art and Design in 1993. She has held solo exhibitions at the Museo de Arte Moderna, São Paulo (2007); The Photographers' Gallery, London (2006); and Fondation Cartier, Paris (2005). She has also participated in group exhibitions at the Contemporary Art Museum, Kumamoto (2016); Centre Pompidou-Merz (2017); and SFMOMA, San Francisco (2016). Kawauchi is the recipient of numerous honours and awards, including the 27th Kimura Ihei Photography Award; the International Centre of Photography Infinity Award; and an Honorary Fellowship of the Royal Photographic Society.

For Rinko Kawauchi

Dear Rinko,

I don't speak Japanese and you don't speak English. Nao had to translate for us. Translation is always a tricky task. How much does it capture and how much gets lost in the process? Is editing occurring? The digital forces us to use language. If we were to sit next to each other I think that you and I would not have any problem communicating. But we cannot be together. I suggest that in order to continue the conversation we use what we are best at – that is, you take photographs and I think about them together with you.

I asked you to tell me about your outside and inside weather. Where are you? At home? Nao sent me your answer:

The weather outside is cloudy.
It's cloudy inside me too.
I am in my studio on the second floor of my house.

Christina Sharpe says that weather is not a meteorological phenomenon but a political and ideological one that affects bodies unevenly. If we understand weather like this we can say that Covid-19 is part of the weather of our present. It is one of the many weathers we actively co-inhabit along with others such as hetero-patriarchy, anti-blackness, racism, the neo-liberal extractivism of our planet, and human bodies.[13] Is your house in a tall building? Do you usually look through the window? Windows seems to be important. What do you see?

13. Astrida Neimanis, 'The Sea and the Breathing,' *e-flux Architecture, e-flux, May 2020.*

It is on the second floor of a two-story building.
There are always trees outside the window and their greenery soothes me.

How did you go through lockdown during the pandemic? What did you do? Did you spend time on your own?

I was at home with my family during the pandemic.

I drove around the neighborhood and found a swallow's nest and photographed it. I made a book of [the photographs] and had it sold by a French publisher. I also continued to take photographs around my home, and the work will be exhibited in a large solo exhibition in Tokyo this October. The production process has not changed, but I can no longer go abroad to shoot.

I wish I could see the swallow's nest. I wonder how you take photographs of swallows' nests. Are you trying to act as a hunter and shoot with your camera? Or are you trying to be still like a tree and learn to breathe otherwise in order not to scare them?

The swallows were wary of me at first, but since I am photographing them all the time, they are becoming less and less concerned.

Can I understand *Cui Cui* as an ongoing series that follows life?

Although *Cui Cui* is complete as a work, I continue to photograph my family, so I may present a sequel one day.

How can the work about family ever be complete? What moments make you think it is complete and ready to start a new chapter?

The theme of the work *Cui Cui* is family, and it is about life and death, cycles, and reincarnation, so the death of my grandfather and the birth of my nephew represent a cycle. I am still photographing my family, and I published a book of photographs of my daughter in 2020 called *as it is*. It is a work of a different character from *Cui Cui*.

(05) Sejin Kim

Sejin Kim (born 1971, Daejeon, South Korea; lives Seoul, South Korea) is a video artist and filmmaker who combines documentary realism with the poetics of cinema to explore the complex entanglement between individuals and the larger political and social systems in which they live. Her work chronicles the contemporary condition, pulling focus to feelings of anxiety and fear, loneliness and alienation, conflict and confusion – feelings that all individuals must endure as we attempt to negotiate our existence in a society that sustains itself by placing limitations on its members.

Kim graduated with a MFA in Fine Art Media from Slade School of Fine Art, University College London, in 2012. Kim has held solo exhibitions at the SongEun Art Space, Seoul (2019); and Prizma Space, Istanbul (2015). Her work has also been exhibited at Frieze No.9 Cork Street, London (2022); the National Museum of Modern and Contemporary Art, Seoul (2021); Nam June Paik Art Center, Seoul (2020); grunt gallery, Vancouver (2019); La Friche, Marseille (2015); and MAXXI, Rome (2014). She was the recipient of the SongEun Art Award in 2016; The 4th Daum Prize in 2005; and the Unesco Prize for the Promotion of the Arts in 2002.

For Sejin Kim

Sejin Kim was in Seoul. She had just moved to a new area of the city. Being alone during the pandemic made her take the step to move closer to her family. The white sofa behind her took on a monumental presence in the room. She took notes and paused often during our conversation.

Dear Sejin Kim,

You told me that the museum is not an ordinary place. You explained that it is a stage. Watching your work *Urban Hermit* and the scenes of empty museums, I couldn't resist connecting it with images of closed museums during the pandemic lockdowns. It reminded me of the initiative *Museums One by One* by Mario García Torres in Mexico and made me think that museums should stay open for individual visits during lockdowns – that as spaces, museums are sanitary and much safer then supermarkets.

During lockdown in Melbourne, I dreamt of going some place other than a supermarket. García Torres suggests that museums should also be healing places that allow you to be alone with artworks for a certain amount of time. I still have a naïve dream that museums can become places of refuge. You told me simply that it is too late for such dreams. I just swallowed my saliva, not knowing what to say. You said that we should stop maintaining museums. But we obviously cannot do that because we are part of the assembly line that continues to keep the system alive through our participation.

You understand the museum as a stage. But a stage for whom? And for what purpose? How do we share that stage with invisible people, guards, cleaning ladies and people on the margins who sustain our system of art-making and whose labour has been, in many cases, invisible to most of us? In recent years, we have witnessed protests, such as *Who keeps the cube white?* organised by the students at Goldsmiths, University of London, which tried to pressure the newly established art center to have in-house rather than outsourced cleaning staff. These protests come and go but what is important is structural change.

You kept telling me that the cleaning lady is so important.

When researchers Kaja Krener and Robert Bobnic interviewed Dr. Dragan R. Milivojević, a researcher and former employee of the Bor Institute of Mining and Metallurgy, about the worker self-management system in the former Yugoslavia, he reflected that:

> The complex organisation of RTB Bor had 23,000 employees. In each relatively autonomous unit of RTB Bor, an

assembly of working people had to happen – an assembly of all the employees – and more than 50% of them [must] vote for this idea. The voice of the lady who [made] coffee and my voice were considered equal. It's funny but it was a reality. [14]

14. Robert Bobnic and Kaja Krener, 'Bor is Burning: Political Economy of IT in Socialist Republic of Yugoslavia,' As you go… roads under your feet towards the new future (2020).

This example of a self-management system from the former Yugoslavia – which was not only implemented in factories but throughout society – is worth exploring. I wonder how many cleaning ladies or guards are invited to participate in curatorial meetings or decision-making in art institutions today.

Biljana Ciric

(06) Pixy Liao

Pixy Liao (born 1979, Shanghai, China; lives New York, USA) uses photography, video, and installation to question stereotypical representations of couples, artists, and the female experience. Although Liao's work is highly personal, she uses wit and humour to explore the dynamics between gender, power, and race. She often portrays herself in a dominant role with her boyfriend assuming a more submissive position in order to break the predominant relationship model and experiment with new modes of being together.

Liao holds an MFA in photography from the University of Memphis. She has held solo exhibitions at Fotografiska, New York and Stockholm (2021); SCOPE Hannover Biennale (2020); and Photoworks Festival, Brighton (2020). She has been included in group shows at M Woods Museum, Beijing (2020); National Gallery of Australia, Canberra (2020); and Rencontres d'Arles (2019). She is a recipient of a NYFA Fellowship in Photography; Santo Foundation Individual Artist Award; Jimei x Arles Madame Figaro Women Photographers Award; En Foco Photography Fellowship; and LensCulture Exposure Awards.

For Pixy Liao

While we were zooming together, Moro was setting the intimacy for the evening by closing the windows behind Pixy. They were in Italy, travelling and learning to live again. I could see Moro's white T-shirt and long, skinny hands partially entering the Zoom square as he shut the curtains. It was evening, around 9:30, after I had put my son to sleep. Pixy's face was soft and relaxed.

Dear Pixy and Moro,

I am writing to you both because you made me think about how you are both equally important for the life you are living and the work you are making. I notice a willingness to participate fully in a relationship and share a beauty that many don't recognise as such.

Moro, when I asked Pixy if there is anything she would like to add at the end of the conversation, you said that it's a challenge to standardise an idea of male beauty. Your last sentence stayed in the air long after the Zoom window closed. It made me think about how the understanding of beauty implicates certain values and norms of gender constructs and sexuality that are products of patriarchy and rooted in the capitalist exploitation of female or male bodies, body performance, labour and its institutionalisation.

Silvia Federici suggests that our acceptance of rules and regulations implies that we accept norms. This involuntary submission is accompanied by an inner injustice and a desire to revolt, which, she suggests, has been formative in determining what *woman* means today, or what man means today, and how gender norms shape us and our relationship to others and the world around us.[15] We have been instructed in detail about how our bodies should look and about how to stay healthy in order to perform our roles and contribute our labour. Following the failure of health systems to perform their duties during the pandemic, we turned even more to these norms, finding refuge in gyms and healthy living as a result of anxieties about what could happen to us if our bodies stop being productive and contributing to the assembly line. Federici points out that to change our body, to regain control over our sexuality and reproductive capacity, is to change the material conditions of our lives.[16] I read, in your work and your relationship, a comfort in taking that control into your own hands every time you take a new photo together.

Paolo Freire said that our incompleteness gives us hope. Our beauty can be found in that very incompleteness. Our unfinishedness foregrounds our movement to search, to learn and to unlearn, and makes our presence ethical – not only in order to adapt to the world but to intervene, to re-create, and to transform it.[17] The more we think of ourselves as complete, finished, whole, the more we cannot love or be loved. [18]

15. Silvia Federici, *Beyond the Periphery of the Skin* (Oakland, CA: PM Press, 2020), 45.

16. Federici, *Beyond the Periphery of the Skin,* 35.

17. Paulo Freire, *Pedagogy of Freedom: Ethics, Democracy and Civic Courage*. Critical Perspectives Series (Lanham, Md.; Oxford: Rowman & Littlefield Publishers, 1998), 56.

18. Stefano Harney and Fred Moten, *All Incomplete* (Colchester: Minor Compositions, 2021), 41.

It struck me that you didn't make any work during the lockdown and, exactly like me, you felt trapped in your own home. You moved to mending broken ceramics, learning techniques for folding paper, feeling that every day was the same. Most of your work happens in the intimate setting of your living environment, but I also understood that many of these places are not your home but rather, friends' houses or Airbnbs that you have stayed in, and that you make work while you travel. Mobility is important both for your relationship and for the work to occur. Travel and mobility are as important as the windows in the photos you take. As you said, windows create a sense of the relationship as light rather than heavy, of looking outside, of connecting the private to the public.[19]

19. Pixy Liao, *in conversation with the author,* May 23, 2022.

Biljana Ciric

(07) Lin Zhipeng (aka No.223)

Lin Zhipeng (aka No.223) (born 1979, Guangdong, China; lives Beijing, China) is a photographer and writer who captures the need to love in an otherwise indifferent society. 223's photographs reflect the zeitgeist of the post-80s and 90s generation of non-mainstream Chinese youth. Amidst an often-closed traditional culture, his photographs act as a collective not-so-private diary of a young generation pushing against the limits of the rigid social rules of conservative Chinese society.

223 graduated from Guangdong University of Foreign Studies, majoring in finance and English. He has held solo exhibitions at Delaware Contemporary Museum (2019); and The Walther Collection, Neu Ulm (2019). 223 has also exhibited at Three Shadows Photography Art Center, Beijing (2018); Xi'an Art Museum (2017); GuatePhoto International Photography Festival, Antigua (2015); 10th Lianzhou International Photography Festival (2014); Shanghai Gallery of Art (2012); and FotoGrafia International Festival, Rome (2008).

For Lin Zhipeng (aka No.233)

He was in Beijing when I reached out. He didn't know that I speak Chinese, so he sent a short sentence to my email before the meeting to say that his English is poor. The outside weather was summer, and his inside weather was also summer. There was something in his attitude towards life that I admired. Something that manifested in that big smile and a sense of lightness from having left troubles behind. Perhaps I admired it because it's an attitude I don't have. I also felt the need to understand whether, deep in his heart, there is a small corner that is heavy and dark and whether that small corner sometimes gets bigger. I didn't want to dig deeper. I wanted to believe in his summer.

Dear 223,

Your practice is usually described as documenting the lives of non-mainstream youth in conservative China. After our conversation today I understood that this is not the case. You are documenting your own life and the lives of your close friends and when you started doing so, you and your friends were young. But you continued to photograph the same people over ten years. You photograph them changing as they grow and get old, as small wrinkles and grey hairs appear. You are documenting life. Youth was just one part of it. Now I know that your focus, instead of being narrow, is life itself, and that is much greater and more powerful.

Who are the people whose bodies we gaze at? Friends, close friends, intimate friends. You only photograph people you are close to. You call them people with crazy ideas and in the photographs we see how they reveal some of these ideas to us. I wonder how you perceive the camera between them and you, what does this object that you are holding in your hand mean and what does it do to your relationships with your subjects when you decide to take a photo? You said that for you, the camera is your third eye. There is a level of violence when we say 'shooting someone' in English because it has a double meaning. It can mean to kill or to take a photo of someone. In the Chinese language 拍照 (taking photo) doesn't have that connotation. Do you feel that you are taking something from them or are you giving them something? What is it that you are taking or giving? Could it be a process that goes in both directions?

You shared with me that you have a short memory, so photos help you remember. Thanks to them you remember details of the moments – their smell, their taste.

I appreciate the strength in your position of not assuming censorship as a struggle and an obstacle. Instead, you find different and more intimate ways to share the work that you do. Your practice is usually defined as erotic or sexually charged. I would like to think of the erotic in different terms – as power. In *Uses of the Erotic: The Erotic as Power*, Audre Lorde explains that the erotic is a resource within each of us that lies in a deeply female and spiritual plane, firmly rooted in the power of unexpressed or unrecognised feelings.[20] Our erotic knowledge empowers us and, as Lorde suggests, becomes a lens through which we scrutinise all aspects of our existence.[21] The erotic is actually the sharing of joy with another person and it can be emotional, intellectual and physical. It is a bridge that allows us to understand what our differences are and to fathom that which is not shared between us. Your work underlines that capacity for joy and power – something that many are afraid of when they face it because they have already settled for convenience.

20. Audre Lorde, *Sister Outsider,* Penguin Classics, 2007, 43.

21. Lorde, *Sister Outsider,* 47.

Your work is political because the personal is political. I look through the photos and I see friends – a community on the margins of society that has created a utopian intimacy through which touch is healing. I see your friends as part of a generation for whom an understanding of the body in relationship with other bodies of humans and more-than-human worlds is emerging. Relationships with a mushroom, a flower or a stone. The joy of sharing emerges from every frame. The joy of a moment that connects us to a larger cycle of time.

Biljana Ciric

[08] Tao Hui

Tao Hui (born 1987, Yunyang, Chongqing, China; lives Beijing, China) works across various mediums including graphic arts, painting, video, objects, and installation. Drawing from personal memories, visual experiences, Chinese tradition and popular culture, Tao Hui creates experimental narrations which focus on our collective experience. By questioning the tenets of globalisation, virtual relationships, and hegemonic thinking, Tao Hui prompts the audience to face their own cultural histories and values.

Tao Hui trained at the Sichuan Fine Arts Institute and graduated with a bachelor's degree in oil painting in 2010. He has presented solo exhibitions at OCAT Xi'an (2017); and UCCA, Beijing (2015). His work has also been exhibited at the Centre d'Art Contemporain Genève (2020); MACRO Asilo, Rome (2019); Museum of Contemporary Art Leipzig (2019); Belem Cultural Center, Lisbon (2018); Centre Pompidou, Paris (2017); Hugo Boss Asia Art Award for Emerging Artists, Rockbund Art Museum, Shanghai (2017); Fondation Louis Vuitton, Paris (2016); Fondazione Museo Pino Pascali, Polignano a Mare (2016); and the 11th Shanghai Biennale (2016). In 2015, Tao Hui was awarded the prestigious Grand Prize at the 19th Contemporary Art Festival Sesc Videobrasil, São Paulo.

For Tao Hui

We spoke Chinese when we met. Tao Hui was in Beijing. He shared the sense of frustration and loneliness that he felt while walking Beijing's empty streets when nothing was open. He had to do daily PCR tests to enter and leave the building. We struggled to imagine what the future of China will look like, and discussed his feeling of being useless as an artist in a situation like this. He said that the pandemic made him closer to his mother and now they understand each other better.

Dear Tao Hui,

In her recent text *Arguments for a New Aesthetic of Presence*, Chiara Cappelletto asks, in relation to quarantine, 'are we not asked to stay in what is, by definition, the most welcoming space for us: our homes? Why then does this space appear so inhospitable to us?'[23] Coming from decades in which mobility was everything, home confinement has suddenly become a cut-off point at which our experience of near and far, neighbour and stranger, collapses… When you talk about this I know you are not only referring to home confinement; even gathering on the riverbank is not welcomed in Beijing, and for the third year in a row, the borders remain closed.

22. Chiara Cappelletto, 'Arguments for a New Aesthetic of Presence', Critical Inquiry, May 2020.

During the 80s and 90s in China and in many other parts of the world, artists' studios and apartments were not only places where things were produced, but also spaces where discourse, gatherings and exhibitions happened. In localities where there were no museums, no infrastructure or no support for experimental practices, these modes of coming together, sharing and discussing art were crucial for artists and the close community. I have been in dialogue with colleagues from Russia lately and I am noticing that diplomats' houses have again become one of the few safe places to gather and to share. I think this was the same in China in the 90s, and I am afraid this situation will return in near futures.

You say that you are discouraged as an artist and you don't see a future. I had the same anxiety when the pandemic started. My most common question to my partner was *what do we do next?* Donald Dwayne reminds us that issues of climate change and sustainability are not problems that science and technology can solve. They are cultural and spiritual problems. We cannot change things by telling people what they should do, but by changing the way they live.[23] The way we live. The way we live as humans and how we practice as humans and artists or curators.

23. Donald Dwayne, 'Homo Economicus and Forgetful Curriculum: Remembering other ways to be a human being', lecture, The Sustainability Council, University of Alberta, YouTube, 23 January 2020.

The Chinese system emphasises harmony and as Trinh T. Minh-ha reminds us, harmony means a certain oppression which does not allow people's everyday life to escape control.[24] For artists, freedom and the everyday are important states where art and life intertwine.

24. *Ute Meta Bauer in conversation with Trinh Thi Min-ha*, CCA, Graduate Program in Curatorial Practice and the Curatorial Research Bureau. Vimeo, 17 October 2019.

I am hoping that collectively we will consider the question: *what are the pedagogies of transition towards different kinds of humans and modes of instituting?*[25] Who can you be and how can you know the world in relation to others? For me, instituting is closely connected to curatorial practice which I understand as a gesture of caring with others, that can collectively lead to more sustainable working methodologies.

25. Rolando Vazquez, *On Social and Climate Justice- Transforming Institution,* Jan van Eyck Academie, 15 November 2021.

I am writing this while acknowledging that you are in China. *What about China?* Trinh T. Minh-ha asks us in the title of her new film.[26] There are many Chinas that we carry within us, not only the abstract name used in mainstream media or the part of a system that imposes restrictions on our being. Whenever we say 'China' we create an 'elsewhere' within here. It is a complex multilayered existence that we all contribute to with every step we take, every word we say. China is also you and your beautiful relationship to your mother that you learnt to enjoy, thanks to the pandemic. Your sharing will also enrich my own China that continues to transform as I reach out towards her.

26. Trinh T. Minh-ha, *What about China?,* 2022, 135 minute film.

Biljana Ciric

(09) Lieko Shiga

Lieko Shiga (born 1980, Aichi, Japan; lives Miyagi, Japan) is a photographer whose practice connects enquiries about the nature of the photographic medium with fundamental questions about life and the means of expressing oneself. Characterised by their intense colour saturation, heavy use of flash and uncanny, dreamlike tone, Shiga's photographs deliberately transgress the conventions of documentary photography, blurring the boundaries between reality and representation, and drawing on local myths and personal accounts.

Shiga graduated with a BA of Fine Art New Media at the Chelsea College of Art and Design, London Institute, in 2004. She has held solo exhibitions at the Tokyo Photographic Art Museum (2019); and Foam Museum, Amsterdam (2013). Her work has been presented at significant institutions, including the 5th Ural Industrial Biennial of Contemporary Art (2019); Haus der Kulturen der Welt, Berlin (2017); Centre Pompidou-Metz (2017); San Francisco Museum of Modern Art (2016); 8th Asia Pacific Triennial Of Contemporary Art, QAGOMA, Brisbane (2015); and Museum of Modern Art, New York (2015). She was awarded the Kimura Ihei Photography Award in 2008; Infinity Award (Young Photographer) from the International Center of Photography, New York in 2009; and the 28th Higashikawa Award (New Photographer) in 2012.

Face

From *R's Boat*,
University of California Press, 2010

Lisa Robertson

A man's muteness runs through this riot that is my sentence.

I am concerned here with the face and hands and snout.

All surfaces stream dark circumstance of utterance.

What can I escape?

Am I also trying to return?

Not the private bucket, not the 7,000 griefs in the bucket of each cold clammy word.

But just as strongly I willed myself towards this neutrality.

I have not loved enough or worked.

What I want to do here is infiltrate sincerity.

I must speak of what actually happens.

Could it be terrible then?

I find abstraction in monotony, only an object, falling.

Gradually the tree came to speak to me.

I heard two centuries of assonance, and then rhyme.

Had I the choice again, I'd enter whole climates superbly indifferent to abstraction.

I saw amazing systems that immediately buckled.

Here I make delicate reference to the Italian goddess Cardea who shuts what is open and opens what is shut.

I conceived of an organ slightly larger than skin, a structure of inhuman love minus nostalgia or time.

Honeysuckle, elder, moss, followed one another like a sequence of phrases in a sentence, distinct, yet contributing successively to an ambience that for the sake of convenience I will call the present.

I experienced a transitive sensation to the left of my mind.

I am concerned here with the face and hands and snout.

Was I a plunderer then?

I am interested in whatever mobilizes and rescues the body.

I saw the sentiment of my era, then published its correspondence.

I am satisfied with so little.

I felt pampered by the austerity—it pushed my hip so I rolled.

I become the person who walks through the door.

The air goes soft and I'm cushioned as by the skin of an animal.

I can only make a report.

Womanliness knows nothing and laughs.

I can't live for leaves, for grass, for animals.

All surfaces stream dark circumstance of utterance.

I can't say any of these words.

Gradually the tree comes to speak to me.

I collaborated with my boredom.

I write this ornament, yet I had not thought of time.

I come to you for information.

Sometimes I'm just solid with anger and I am certain I will die from it.

I conceived of an organ slightly larger than skin, a structure of inhuman love
minus nostalgia or time.

If only I could achieve frankness.

I could be quiet enough to hear the culverts trickling.

I'm talking about weird morphing catalogues and fugitive glances.

I could have been wrong.

I subsist by these glances.

I desire nothing humble or abridged.

I'm using the words of humans to say what I want to know.

I did not sigh.

I confined my thievery to perishable items.

I do not want to speak partially.

I loosened across landscape.

I doubt that I am original.

I've been lucky and I'm thankful.

I dreamt I lied.

I stole butter and I studied love.

Something delighted me.

And if I am not cherished?

I endlessly close.

But just as strongly I willed myself towards this neutrality.

I enjoyed that pleasure I now inhabit.

I collaborated with my boredom.

I experienced a transitive sensation to the left of my mind.

I stood in the horizontal and vertical cultures of words like a bar in a graph.

I feel like the city itself should confess.

With the guilt that I quietly believe anything, I dreamt I lied.

I felt pampered by the austerity—it pushed my hip so I rolled.

I desire nothing humble or abridged.

I find abstraction in monotony, only an object, falling.

Yet I enjoyed sex in the shortening seasons.

I had at my disposal my feet and my lungs and these slimnesses.

I am satisfied with so little.

I had insisted on my body's joy and little else.

I wish not to judge or to dawdle.

I had no plan but to advance into Saturday.

I had a sense that I'd strengthen, and speak less.

It was a chic ideal.

Look, I'm stupid and desperate and florid with it.

I have a figure of it.

Had I the choice again, I'd enter whole climates superbly indifferent to
abstraction.

I have been like lyric.

I withdrew from all want and all knowledge.

I have myself defined the form and the vulnerability of this empiricism.

I heard that death is the work of vocables towards silence.

I have no complaints.

I could have been wrong.

I have not loved enough or worked.

I have myself defined the form and the vulnerability of this empiricism.

I have nothing to say.

I come to you for information.

I burn, I blurt, I am sure to forget.

In the evening I walked through the terrific solidity of fragrance, not memory.

I heard that death is the work of vocables towards silence.

Honeysuckle, elder, moss, followed one another like a sequence of phrases
in a sentence, contributing successively to an ambience that for the sake
of convenience I will call the present.

I heard two centuries of assonance, and then rhyme.

I may have been someone who was doing nothing more than studying the
Norman flax bloom.

I let myself write these sentences.

I needed history in order to explain myself.

I loosened across landscape.

I raised my voice to say No!

I made my way to London.

I made my way to London.

I must speak of our poverty in the poem.

I can't live for leaves, for grass, for animals.

I must speak of what actually happens—

I'm a popstar and this is how I feel.

I only know one thing: I, who allots her fickle rights.

I feel like the city itself should confess.

I only wanted to live on apples, in a meadow, with quiet.

I can only make a report.

I permit myself to be led to the other room.

I have nothing to say, I burn, I blurt, I am sure to forget.

I preserved solitude as if it were a style.

I am ignorant, but I know.

I raised my voice to say No!

I was almost the absolute master.

I saw amazing systems that immediately buckled.

I enjoyed that pleasure I now inhabit.

I slept like these soft trees.

I'm wondering about the others, the dead I love.

I speak as if to you alone.

Am I also trying to return?

I stood in the horizontal and vertical cultures of words like a bar in a graph.

I can't say any of these words.

I subsist by these glances.

Still I don't know what memory is.

I think of it now as mine.

Here I make delicate reference to the Italian goddess Cardea who shuts what is open and opens what is shut.

I took part in large-scale erotic digressions.

The present has miscalculated me.

I want to mention the hammered fastenings in ordinary speech.

I want to mention the hammered fastenings in ordinary speech.

I was willing to suppose that there existed nothing really.

But what I want to do here is infiltrate sincerity.

I was wrong.

I'm for the flickering effect in vernaculars.

I will construct men or women.

I had insisted on my body's joy and little else.

I will not remember, only transcribe.

This is the first time I've really wanted to be accurate.

I will write about time, patience, compromise, weather, breakage.

I sleep like these soft trees in sleep are sweeping me.

I wish not to judge or to dawdle.

I took part in large-scale erotic digressions.

I wished to think about all that was false.

I'm really this classical man.

I withdrew from all want and all knowledge.

In the strange shops and streets I produce this sign of spoken equilibrium.

I write this ornament, yet I had not thought of rhyme.

This is emotional truth.

I'm crying love me more.

Its landscapes are cemeteries.

I'm just a beam of light or something.

I only know one thing: I, who allots her fickle rights.

I'm using the words of humans to say what I want to know.

I did not sigh.

I'm wondering about the others, the dead I love.

I only wanted to live on apples, in a meadow, with quiet.

If only I could achieve frankness.

I had no plan but to advance into Saturday.

In the evening I walked through the terrific solidity of fragrance, not memory.

Life appeared quite close to me.

In the strange shops and streets I produce this sign of spoken equilibrium.

I could be quiet enough to hear the culverts trickling.

In the year of my physical perfection I took everything literally.

Still, the problem was not my problem.

It was the period in which ordinary things became possible.

I am interested in whatever mobilizes and rescues the body.

Life appeared quite close to me.

I will construct men or women.

Limbs, animals, utensils, stars

I crave extension.

Look, I'm stupid and desperate and florid with it.

I do not want to speak partially.

My freedom was abridged.

I speak as if to you alone.

O, to quietly spend money.

I let myself write these sentences.

Of course later I will understand my misconceptions.

I doubt that I am original.

Sometimes I'm just solid with anger.

I have been like lyric.

Still, I don't know what memory is.

I have a chic ideal.

Such is passivity.

I will not remember, only transcribe.

Lisa Robertson

Lisa Robertson is a Canadian poet, essayist and translator.

To Sleep, Perchance to Work: The Temporality of Un/Employment in Shunji Iwai's *A Bride for Rip Van Winkle*

Kelley Dong

Even a soul submerged in sleep is hard at work, and helps make something of the world.
— Heraclitus, Fragments[1]

At the onset of the Covid-19 pandemic, attrition soared across the United Kingdom and the United States. Though resignation and unemployment rates did not reach record heights in countries like Australia, India, Japan, and Canada, nonetheless a perceptible ripple of dissatisfaction spread across the global labour pool.[2] These shifts indicated the start of a mass revelation among workers about the very meaning and value of work – a turn away from what Paul Lafargue describes as Christian and capitalist ethics, which enforce a stultifying love of work against 'the pleasures of idleness'.[3] Faced with inflation, supply shortages, pay cuts, inflexible work schedules, and a lack of health and unemployment benefits, many could no longer lie about possessing an intrinsic desire to work.

Some publicised their apostasy by sharing images and videos of themselves walking off the job or telling off their employers. For example, in a widely circulated video, Shana Blackwell announces into a Walmart intercom: 'This company treats their employees like shit… I fucking quit.' [4] She then exits the store, leaving behind her minimum wage job as a night stocker. Others, like the members of the Reddit forum r/antiwork (who refer to themselves as 'idlers'), began exchanging tales of workplace disillusionment and anti-work enlightenment.

Though commiseration among disparately located individuals might seem minutely effectual as collective anti-capitalist action, it provokes a capitalist hostility against anyone who does not dream of or live to work. (Consider the question posed by Fox News host Jesse Watters to r/antiwork moderator Doreen Ford, 'Why do you like the idea of being home, not working, but still getting paid by corporate America?'[5]) This antagonism refuses the relief afforded by the liminal temporality of unemployment, which emulsifies leisure and precarity. For the enervated worker, the sudden abundance of free time gained via unemployment restores what Marx described as 'time for growth, development, and healthy maintenance of the body… the time required for the consumption of fresh air and sunlight' stolen by the workday.[6]

One of unemployment's paradoxical pleasures is that the separation of productivity from salaried time elongates every second, minute and hour, thus generating more time to uncover different forms of productivity. In *Girls of the Night*, 1961, Kinuyo Tanaka distinguishes between weeks of employment and hours of unemployment according to the extent of mental agency permitted and exercised. After Japan's passing of the 1956 Prostitution Prevention Law, which mandated the arrest and forced rehabilitation of sex workers, Kuniko (Chisako Hara) exits a reformatory and re-enters the workforce as a housekeeper for a grocer's family. The severe demands of the job include what Kuniko can and cannot do in her free time. She must wash her clothes separately

1. Heraclitus. *Fragments*. Translated by Brooks Haxton. (New York: Penguin Books, 2003), 57.

2. Julia Horowitz, 'The Great Resignation is taking root around the world,' CNN, 30 March 2022.

3. Paul Lefargue, 'Blessings of Work,' in *The Right to Be Lazy and Other Studies*, trans. Charles Kerr (Chicago: Charles H. Kerr & Company Co-operative, 1883).

4. Shana Blackwell (@shanablackwell), 'And here is the video of me quitting my toxic, sexist, racist workplace. #walmartchallenge #fyp #viral #walmart #walmarthaul #walmartfindspart1', TikTok, 30 October 2020.

5. Joshua Needelman, 'Like a bully in the schoolyard, Fox News sets its sights on the anti-work movement,' The Guardian, 1 February 2022.

6. Karl Marx, 'The Struggle for a Normal Working-Day. Compulsory Laws for the Extension of the Working-Day from the Middle of the 14th to the End of the 17th Century,' in *Capital*, Volume 1, trans. Samuel Moore and Edward Aveling (1867; repr. Ware: Wordsworth Edition Limited, 2013), 183.

and clean the washroom after she bathes; when she steals away for a break, she is harassed by male employees and bombarded by requests made by the grocer's wife. The workdays bleed into one another as one endless shift, until Kuniko reaches that common conclusion among workers: 'I do not get paid enough for this'. She quits her job, leaves the grocery store, and takes a stroll through the city. Tanaka – herself a prolific director and actress who starred in over 250 films throughout her career with few breaks between productions – cuts between Kuniko and the men and women who pass her by, walking hand in hand. She furrows her brow, deep in concentration. Could these couples be lovers, spouses, or sex workers with their johns? Which of these futures lies in store for her? Though this desperate question looms over Kuniko, these concerns are held at bay by a cup of coffee and a few important hours of thinking without being monitored.

In many ways, Shunji Iwai's *A Bride for Rip Van Winkle*, 2016, can be seen as a spiritual successor to Tanaka's Girls of the Night. Both films structure their female protagonists' pursuit of autonomy around a series of jobs, and both – more in the spirit of romantic individualism than anti-capitalism – depict the state of joblessness as equally significant to that of employment. There are three versions of *Rip Van Winkle*: a two-hour version for international audiences, a three-hour director's cut, and a four-and-a-half-hour version for Japanese television. The film's characters possess a similar multiplicity, having made themselves polymorphous to meet the demands of the market. Each has several part-time and full-time jobs, many of which are never explicitly named, and sometimes work anonymously or pseudonymously. Over the course of *Rip Van Winkle* one gleans that most of these workers were hired through social media, specifically on the fictional platform Planet. The fantastical frequency with which these jobs appear and disappear demystifies work by diminishing the myth of a perfect and permanent job, thereby separating purpose from employment.

At the start of *Rip Van Winkle*, protagonist Nanami (Haru Koroki) appears to live obligatorily and not willingly, as if she has been employed by life. The film opens on an intersection, much like the one Kuniko finds herself in in *Girls of the Night*, where one cannot easily differentiate between transactional and non-transactional encounters. Here, Nanami – a part-time teacher, tutor, and grocery clerk – has arranged to meet her online acquaintance Tetsuya (Gō Jobiki) in person for the first time. The scene consists only of wide shots of the pair from afar and extreme closeups of text messages, thus usurping any materiality or intimacy. (On Planet, Nanami later confesses that she finds online dating 'way too easy, like I was shopping online … with just one click'.) The events that follow – Nanami and Tetsuya's courtship, engagement, and marriage – proceed expeditiously with neither friction nor passion. Marriage joins Nanami's extant roster of jobs as she tries to win the approval of her husband's middle-class family. She lies about her parents' divorce, hires actors (via Planet) to attend the wedding as family members, and eventually quits her jobs to be a stay-at-home wife. Despite Nanami's efforts, her mother-in-law requests a divorce on her son's behalf. Much like a layoff, this forced exit involves a negative performance feedback, paperwork, and packed boxes.

Homeless, jobless, and penniless, Nanami heads out with a large suitcase in tow. She moves in slow-motion, the camera swivelling around her as she faces every direction with uncertainty. The composition recalls Jeff Wall's photograph *Overpass*, 2001, the title of which refers both to the actual overpass in the image and a transitory state. It cannot be determined where the subjects came from, where they may be headed, or whether their plastic bags and suitcases carry entire lives' worth of belongings. The movement of the Steadicam adds to this image of suspension a discombobulating effect reminiscent of the unpredictable nature of being a worker in the twenty-first century gig economy: sometimes there is work, sometimes there is none.

Rip Van Winkle integrates Steadicam footage in nearly every scene, and frequently the footage included demonstrates a counter-intuitive use of the Steadicam. For instance, rather than obscure the fact of the manual grip held by the camera operator by including only shots with smooth motion, *Rip Van Winkle* has many shots in which the Steadicam tilts out of orbit or becomes jolted and obstructed by people and objects that are fully visible in the frame. Unlike the films of Terrence Malick, in which the Steadicam drifts as if it were led by the divine logic of a heavenly gaze, *Rip Van Winkle* makes the viewer especially sensitive to the possibility of risk and destruction that lies in every manoeuvre. (This unease is compounded by the film's dim lighting, which blurs detail and compels the viewer to strain and squint.)

Yet dire circumstances awaken Nanami's dormant desire to live. Living off meagre wages and convenience-store snacks, she finds work as a hotel maid. She continues to be a part-time virtual tutor as well, much to the delight of her one student. An enigmatic Planet friend, Amuro (Gō Ayano), arranges for Nanami to work as a wedding attendee – the same service she previously enlisted. At her first wedding gig, Nanami meets workers like herself, each introducing themselves with a fake name. But like any family that partakes in a day's work of cordiality for the sake of keeping up appearances at a wedding, the closeness felt between the co-workers dissipates almost as soon as it takes form. Nanami and fellow attendee Mashiro (Cocco) exchange names and Planet handles – Mashiro's Planet username is Rip Van Winkle – before Mashiro vanishes without warning, likely to work another shift at a different job. Mashiro's departure leaves Nanami to wonder alone what work will look like tomorrow.

A general malaise is diffused across Iwai's *All About Lily Chou-Chou*, 2001, which traces a network of teenagers who interact through a fan website dedicated to the musician Lily Chou-Chou. With regards to these adolescents, the film's very lack of a diagnosis functions as its broad thesis: youthhood alienates youth, violence begets more violence. Though perhaps not as formally multifaceted, Rip Van Winkle demonstrates more ideological precision. The film avoids being polysemous in its invocation of loneliness by depicting, by way of Marx, how workers alienated from their own labour become alienated from themselves and from one another. In *All About Lily Chou-Chou*, for example, online messages and posts appear as onscreen text against a black background. The distillation of these statements likens the users to members of a Greek chorus who speak simultaneously but not necessarily in conversation. In contrast, *Rip Van Winkle* includes Nanami's phone in the frame, filled with text messages sent and posts made with little or no reply. Unlike the poetic opacity of superimposed text in *Lily Chou-Chou*, these close-ups confirm Nanami's unmet desire to be seen – specifically, to be read – which she projects into a void.

Ken Lum, in his series *Time. And Again*, 2021, makes a similar connection between thought and text. *Time. And Again* is a series of photographs depicting people in public spaces – parks, sidewalks, benches, playgrounds – accompanied by short texts. Each text relates to the theme of time and work during the Covid-19 pandemic, such as the act of waiting for 'a call to work' or 'looking for work', or feeling lucky to have a job at all. And as in Lum's *Portrait-Repeated Text* series, 1993, the relation between text and image indicates that these words derive from the mind of the subject. The most striking of these, entitled *They have no idea how much I work*, depicts a Black woman standing in a playground. Her feet are planted in the sand. She is pushing a child on a swing, whose face is turned away from the camera. The woman looks to her left, facing a bright light that shines in from beyond the frame, towards an object the spectator cannot see. The direction of her gaze recalls Italian neorealist films like those of Vittorio De Sica (such as *Bicycle Thieves*, 1948 and *Umberto D.*, 1952), in which the tracking shot trails behind or beside the character to imbue the scene with the density of the unknown that lies ahead. (In these films, whether the character knows the destination to be an employment office or a factory, there is no guarantee that a job awaits.) The accompanying text of the photograph states: 'They have no idea how hard I work … They have no idea what I do'. The distinction made between 'working' and 'doing' separates the question of whether or not the subject has a job from the truth that the subject is working. Or rather, Lum shows that in capitalism, even an unemployed person is hard at work.

Like Kuniko in *Girls of the Night*, Nanami is recruited, in *Rip Van Winkle*, by Amuro to be a live-in maid for an unknown benefactor. The dusty and filthy mansion where she stays, and which she must clean, initially seems to be a worker's utopia. The pay is exorbitantly high, the fridge is always full, and the boss, Mashiro, is never around. When not working as an actress and model, Mashiro, too, cleans the mansion. But even this flexible and comfortable arrangement reveals itself to be as straightforward as any other job. Nanami discovers that Mashiro – in fact, a terminally ill porn actress – has taken on an excruciating amount of physically demanding work to pay for Nanami's companionship and to rent the mansion under the name of Rip Van Winkle. (One is reminded of Count Dracula's obsession with moving to England, which impels him to purchase property in London and entrap the solicitor Jonathan Harker as an interlocutor between himself and British society.)

The overworked Mashiro's Pyrrhic victory worsens her condition. She looks as if she has already died. Sweat glues strands of hair to her forehead, her face becomes increasingly pale as she falls in and out of consciousness. As in *Dracula*, in which the Count's derelict mansion consumes Harker, Rip Van Winkle's mansion dissolves the boundaries between work and personal life. There are few visitors, and even fewer neighbours. Professional obligations leave Harker with little choice but to stay in the Count's mansion; but it is ultimately admiration, braided with curiosity and fear, that delays Harker's escape. Likewise, Nanami refuses to leave Mashiro's side, though she eventually finds the courage to inform Mashiro that she'd like to quit her job. Nanami proposes that they move away somewhere, 'instead of a mansion like this … a room for the two of us. Even if we're poor'. But the conclusion of Nanami and Mashiro's relationship as employee and employer does not signify the start of an equality between the women as lovers. In fact, *Rip Van Winkle* shows that the removal of financial incentive makes Mashiro and Nanami's union even more fragile. Both must learn what it means to think of love without debt. This shift in perspective comes easier to Nanami than Mashiro.

Iwai compresses Nanami and Mashiro's love affair into one day, the day after Nanami has quit her job as Rip Van Winkle's maid. It is a day when neither Nanami nor Mashiro is working, and neither has any work lined up. They look at potential apartments where they might live together, then enter a bridal boutique. After they try on dresses for a free photoshoot offered by the store clerk, a second wedding sequence begins. Unlike Nanami's meticulously staged and structured wedding with Tetsuya (or the weddings which Nanami and Mashiro attended as actors), here there are neither real nor fake family members. There are no costs, no legal recognition (gay marriage is illegal in Japan), and no rings. Instead, Nanami and Mashiro mime the action of sliding a ring onto each other's fingers on an empty altar. The wedding's omission of capitalist, religious, and heteronormative rituals renders it a ceremony dedicated to the idea of love itself. It needs only to be real for the lovers.

Overwhelmed by Nanami's sincerity, Mashiro confesses that receiving kindness without paying for it makes her feel ashamed. Her statement demonstrates the extent to which work, for Mashiro, functions as a substitute for self-worth: to pay for kindness means that one never needs to consider whether it is deserved, and needs only to work long and hard enough to afford its price. Mashiro's rejection of free things – symptomatic of a work ethic prized by capitalism – circumscribes the parameters of pleasure that she allows herself to feel in her last days. Frightened by love and intimidated by freedom, Mashiro falls asleep clutching a venomous cone snail. By the next morning, she has died.

Despite the continuing stream of one devastation after another, it is evident that Nanami has emerged as the happiest character in the film – happier than Mashiro, happier than Amuro, happier than Tetsuya. Though she is just as quiet as before, one perceives in Nanami a latent strength in the way she does not crumble and instead glides from one job to another, in search of a meaning that can't be found in work itself. From firings, resignations, divorce and death arise opportunities to choose life again and again, and to measure time differently.

In an interview with Roger Ebert, Hayao Miyazaki defines the Japanese concept of 'ma' as the gap in between each clap of his hands.[7] Invoking this meaning of 'ma', *Rip Van Winkle* suggests that the lapses of unemployment or precarious employment – the gaps between jobs, like those on one's resume – are more important for a life fully lived than the time one spends working. Shortly after Mashiro's funeral, Nanami moves into an apartment. She prepares for another virtual tutoring session – her one consistent source of income, albeit a small one. In the final shot of the film, she gently holds her finger, where the invisible ring remains. Its palpable trace proves that just a day of rest with one's lover yields more joy than a lifetime of work.

7. Roger Ebert, 'Hayao Miyazaki Interview', RogerEbert.com, September 12, 2002 https://www.rogerebert.com/interviews/hayao-miyazaki-interview.

Kelley Dong

Kelley Dong is a Toronto-based writer, producer, and filmmaker.

I have not loved enough (or worked) is the second title in the publication series 'Unclaimed Ideas' published by the Simon Lee Foundation Institute of Contemporary Asian Art.

This publication is linked to the exhibition *I have not loved (enough or worked)* at The Art Gallery of Western Australia, Boorloo, from 18 November 2021 to 23 April 2023.

This publication was made possible thanks to the financial support of the Simon Lee Foundation; the Australian Government through the Australia-Japan Foundation and the Australia-Korea Foundation of the Department of Foreign Affairs and Trade; and the Australia Council for the Arts, its arts funding and advisory body; Wesfarmers; and The Art Gallery of Western Australia Foundation.

Curated and edited by Rachel Cieśla
Authors: Mira Asriningtyas, Rachel Cieśla, Biljana Ciric, Kelley Dong and Lisa Robertson
Copy Editor: Kay Campbell, The Comma Institute
Design: Ruolan Xi (@unax.lab) and
Marco Dalle Fratte (@marcodallefratte)
Installation views by Julie Hrnčířová, p. 36-37
Printed in Australia by Peachy Print, Sydney
Published and distributed by The Art Gallery of Western Australia and Mousse Publishing

The Art Gallery of Western Australia
PO Box 8363, Perth Business Centre
Perth, Western Australia 6849
Australia
T + 61 8 9492 6600
admin@artgallery.wa.gov.au
artgallery.wa.gov.au

Mousse Publishing
Contrappunto s.r.l.
Via Pier Candido Decembrio 28
20137, Milan
Italy

Available through:
Mousse Publishing, Milan
moussemagazine.it
DAP | Distributed Art Publishers, New York
artbook.com
Les presses du réel, Dijon
lespressesdureel.com
Antenne Books, London
antennebooks.com

First edition: 2022
ISBN: 9781922868015 The Art Gallery of Western Australia /
9788867495672 Mousse Publishing
€ 22 / $ 25